EH40/2005 Workplace exposure limits

Containing the list of workplace exposure
limits for use with the Control of Substances
Hazardous to Health Regulations 2002
(as amended)

London: TSO

a Williams Lea company

Published by TSO (The Stationery Office), part of Williams Lea, and available from:

Online
https://books.hse.gov.uk/

Mail, Telephone, Fax & E-mail
TSO
PO Box 29, Norwich, NR3 1GN
Telephone orders/General enquiries: 0333 202 5070
Fax orders: 0333 202 5080
E-mail: customer.services@tso.co.uk
Textphone 0333 202 5077

TSO@Blackwell and other Accredited Agents

Printed in the United Kingdom for The Stationery Office.
J003681266 c3 06/20

EH40/2005 contains some material which is legally binding. The Control of Substances Hazardous to Health Regulations 2002 impose requirements by reference to Table 1 of EH40/2005 and the Notices of Approval, which are therefore legally binding. Thus, if Table 1 or the Notices of Approval apply to your work activities, health and safety inspectors will expect you to be complying with these requirements and will, if necessary, take appropriate enforcement action.

The remainder of EH40/2005 is guidance.

This guidance is issued by the Health and Safety Executive. Following the guidance is not compulsory and you are free to take other action. But if you do follow the guidance you will normally be doing enough to comply with the law. Health and safety inspectors seek to secure compliance with the law and may refer to this guidance as illustrating good practice.

CONTENTS

FOREWORD

This 2020 edition replaces the previous version as published in 2018. This edition takes account of the new and amended occupational exposure limits.

New and revised workplace exposure limits (WELs) in force from January 2020

The Health and Safety Executive has approved new and revised workplace exposure limits (WELs).

Details of the changes that came into force on 17 January 2020 can be summarised as follows.

There were new or revised entries for the following substances:

- Hardwood dusts (including mixed dusts)
- Chromium (VI) compounds
- Refractory ceramic fibres
- Respirable crystalline silica
- Vinyl chloride monomer
- Ethylene oxide
- 1,2-Epoxypropane
- Acrylamide
- 2-Nitropropane
- O-Toluidine
- 1,3-Butadiene
- Hydrazine
- Bromoethylene

New skin notations have been added for the following substances:

- Ethylene oxide

The following substances required reductions to the existing WELs:

- Hardwood dusts
- Chromium (VI) compounds
- Refractory ceramic fibres
- Vinyl chloride monomer
- Ethylene oxide
- 1,2-Epoxypropane
- Acrylamide
- 2-Nitropropane
- O-Toluidine
- 1,3-Butadiene
- Hydrazine

INTRODUCTION

1   Many people are exposed to a variety of substances at work (eg chemicals, fumes, dusts, fibres) which can, under some circumstances, have a harmful effect on their health. These are called 'hazardous substances'. If exposure to a hazardous substance is not properly controlled it may cause ill health in a number of ways. The substance may cause harm by:

- too much being taken into the body through breathing;
- being absorbed through the skin;
- being swallowed; or
- acting directly on the body at the point of contact, eg the skin.

2   Some illnesses caused by exposure to hazardous substances in the workplace (occupational diseases) may not appear until a long time after the first exposure. Therefore, it is important to know in advance how to protect the health of people working with hazardous substances and also of other people who may be affected by the work being carried out.

Workplace exposure limits (WELs)

3   WELs are British occupational exposure limits and are set in order to help protect the health of workers. WELs are concentrations of hazardous substances in the air, averaged over a specified period of time, referred to as a time-weighted average (TWA). Two time periods are generally used:

- long-term (8 hours); and
- short-term (15 minutes).

4   Short-term exposure limits (STELs) are set to help prevent effects such as eye irritation, which may occur following exposure for a few minutes.

WELs and the Control of Substances Hazardous to Health Regulations 2002 (as amended) (COSHH)

5   Substances that have been assigned a WEL are subject to the requirements of COSHH.[1] These regulations require employers to prevent or control exposure to hazardous substances. For further information go to www.hse.gov.uk/coshh. Under COSHH, control is defined as adequate only if a) the principles of good control practice are applied, b) any WEL is not exceeded, and c) exposure to asthmagens, carcinogens and mutagens are reduced to as low as is reasonably practicable.

6   The absence of a substance from the list of WELs does not indicate that it is safe. For these substances, exposure should be controlled to a level to which nearly all the working population could be exposed, day after day at work, without any adverse effects on health.

7   As part of the assessment required under regulation 6 of COSHH, employers should determine their own working practices and in-house standards for control of exposure. In some cases, there may be sufficient information available for employers to set an 'in-house' working standard, eg from manufacturers and suppliers of the substance, from publications of industry associations, and from occupational medicine and hygiene journals.

Employees and the self-employed

8   There are also some duties for employees and the self-employed under COSHH; further guidance is given in *The Control of Substances Hazardous to Health Regulations 2002 (as amended). Approved Code of Practice and guidance.*[2]

9   An individual working under an employer's control and direction may be treated as 'self-employed' for tax and national insurance purposes; however, they may be an 'employee' for health and safety purposes and appropriate action must be taken to protect them.

10   If you do not wish to employ workers on this basis, you should seek legal advice. Ultimately, each case can only be decided on its own merits by a court of law.

General Data Protection Regulation

11   Employers, in complying with the requirements of regulation 11 of COSHH, may be required to hold health surveillance records on their employees. The General Data Protection Regulation[3] places requirements on those who hold personal data such as health surveillance records. Further information is available from the Information Commissioner's Office www.ico.org.uk.

LIST OF WORKPLACE EXPOSURE LIMITS (WELS)

12   The system of nomenclature for the substances listed below is based mainly on the convention adopted by the International Union of Pure Applied Chemistry (IUPAC). Where this is not the case, the substances will be flagged:

■   INN International Non-proprietary Name;

■   ISO International Organization for Standardization.

13   For the purposes of these limits, respirable dust and inhalable dust are those fractions of airborne dust which will be collected when sampling is undertaken in accordance with the methods described in MDHS14/4 *General methods for sampling and gravimetric analysis or respirable, thoracic and inhalable aerosols.*[4]

14   Where no specific short-term exposure limit is listed, a figure three times the long-term exposure limit should be used.

Annotations

BMGVs   Biological monitoring guidance values. These are listed in Table 2.

Carc   Capable of causing cancer and/or heritable genetic damage. See paragraphs 48-51.

Sen   Capable of causing occupational asthma. See paragraphs 53-56.

Sk   Can be absorbed through the skin. The assigned substances are those for which there are concerns that dermal absorption will lead to systemic toxicity.

TABLE 1: LIST OF APPROVED WORKPLACE EXPOSURE LIMITS

15   This list is legally binding, as it reproduces the list of workplace exposure limits (WELs) which have been approved by the Health and Safety Executive. The limits are given in ppm and mg.m^{-3}. The conversion method is given in paragraphs 68-69. The Control of Substances Hazardous to Health Regulations 2002 impose requirements by reference to this list.

16   However, the entries in the column headed 'CAS number' are not part of the approved list of WELs. The WELs of the dusts included in the list below refer to the inhalable dust fraction, unless otherwise stated.

| Substance | CAS number | Workplace exposure limit | | | | Comments |
| | | Long-term exposure limit (8-hr TWA reference period) | | Short-term exposure limit (15-minute reference period) | | The Carc, Sen and Sk notations are not exhaustive. |
		ppm	mg.m^{-3}	ppm	mg.m^{-3}	
Acetaldehyde	75-07-0	20	37	50	92	Carc
Acetic acid	64-19-7	10	25	20	50	
Acetic anhydride	108-24-7	0.5	2.5	2	10	
Acetone	67-64-1	500	1210	1500	3620	
Acetonitrile	75-05-8	40	68	60	102	
o-Acetylsalicylic acid	50-78-2	-	5	-	-	
Acrylaldehyde (Acrolein)	107-02-8	0.02	0.05	0.05	0.12	
Acrylamide	79-06-1	-	0.1	-	-	Carc, Sk
Acrylic acid		10	29	20*	59*	*STEL in relation to a 1-minute reference period
Acrylonitrile	107-13-1	2	4.4	-	-	Carc, Sk
Allyl alcohol	107-18-6	2	4.8	4	9.7	Sk
Aluminium alkyl compounds		-	2	-	-	
Aluminium metal inhalable dust respirable dust	7429-90-5	- -	 10 4	- -	- -	
Aluminium oxides inhalable dust respirable dust	1344-28-1	- -	 10 4	- -	- -	
Aluminium salts, soluble		-	2	-	-	
2-Aminoethanol	141-43-5	1	2.5	3	7.6	Sk
Amitrole	61-82-5	-	0.2	-	-	
Ammonia, anhydrous	7664-41-7	25	18	35	25	
Ammonium chloride, fume	12125-02-9	-	10	-	20	
Ammonium sulphamidate	7773-06-0	-	10	-	20	
Aniline	62-53-3	1	4	-	-	Sk
Antimony and compounds except stibine (as Sb)		-	0.5	-	-	
ρ-Aramid respirable fibres	26125-61-1	0.5 fibres/ ml	-	-	-	

Substance	CAS number	Workplace exposure limit				Comments
		Long-term exposure limit (8-hr TWA reference period)		Short-term exposure limit (15-minute reference period)		The Carc, Sen and Sk notations are not exhaustive.
		ppm	mg.m^{-3}	ppm	mg.m^{-3}	
Arsenic and arsenic compounds except arsine (as As)		-	0.1	-	-	Carc
Arsine	7784-42-1	0.05	0.16	-	-	
Asphalt, petroleum fumes	8052-42-4	-	5	-	10	
Azodicarbonamide	123-77-3	-	1.0	-	3.0	Sen
Barium compounds, soluble (as Ba)		-	0.5	-	-	
Barium sulphate inhalable dust respirable dust	7727-43-7	- -	10 4	- -	- -	
Benzene	71-43-2	1	3.25	-	-	Carc, Sk
Benzyl butyl phthalate	85-68-7	-	5	-	-	
Benzyl chloride	100-44-7	0.5	2.6	1.5	7.9	Carc
Beryllium and beryllium compounds (as Be)		-	0.002	-	-	Carc
Bis(2-ethylhexyl) phthalate	117-81-7	-	5	-	10	
Bis(chloromethyl) ether	542-88-1	0.001	0.005	-	-	Carc
Bisphenol A	80-05-7	-	2	-	-	
Bornan-2-one	77-22-2	2	13	3	19	
Boron tribromide	10294-33-4	-	-	1	10	
Bromacil (ISO)	314-40-9	1	11	2	22	
Bromine	7726-95-6	0.1	0.66	0.2	1.3	
Bromoethylene	593-60-2	1	4.4	-	-	Carc
Bromomethane	74-83-9	5	20	15	59	Sk
Butane	106-97-8	600	1450	750	1810	Carc, (only applies if Butane contains more than 0.1% of buta-1,3-diene)
But-2-yne-1,4-diol	110-65-6	-	0.5	-	-	
Buta-1,3-diene	106-99-0	1	2.2	-	-	Carc
Butan-1-ol	71-36-3	-	-	50	154	Sk
Butan-2-ol	78-92-2	100	308	150	462	
Butan-2-one (methyl ethyl ketone)	78-93-3	200	600	300	899	Sk, BMGV
2-Butoxyethanol	111-76-2	25	123	50	246	Sk, BMGV
2-(2-Butoxyethoxy) ethanol	112-34-5	10	67.5	15	101.2	
2-Butoxyethyl acetate	112-07-2	20	133	50	332	Sk
n-Butyl acrylate	141-32-2	1	5	5	26	
n-Butyl chloroformate	592-34-7	1	5.7	-	-	
sec-Butyl acetate	105-46-4	200	966	250	1210	
tert-Butyl acetate	540-88-5	200	966	250	1210	
Butyl acetate	123-86-4	150	724	200	966	
Butyl lactate	138-22-7	5	30	-	-	
2-sec-Butylphenol	89-72-5	5	31	-	-	Sk
Cadmium and cadmium compounds except cadmium oxide fume, cadmium sulphide and cadmium sulphide pigments (as Cd)		-	0.025	-	-	Carc (cadmium metal, cadmium chloride, fluoride and sulphate)
Cadmium oxide fume (as Cd)	1306-19-0	-	0.025	-	0.05	Carc

Substance	CAS number	Workplace exposure limit				Comments
		Long-term exposure limit (8-hr TWA reference period)		Short-term exposure limit (15-minute reference period)		The Carc, Sen and Sk notations are not exhaustive.
		ppm	mg.m^{-3}	ppm	mg.m^{-3}	
Cadmium sulphide and cadmium sulphide pigments (respirable dust (as Cd))		-	0.03	-	-	Carc (cadmium sulphide)
Caesium hydroxide	21351-79-1	-	2	-	-	
Calcium carbonate inhalable dust respirable	1317-65-3	- -	10 4	- -	- -	
Calcium cyanamide	156-62-7	-	0.5	-	1	
Calcium hydroxide	1305-62-0	-	5 1	-	- 4	Respirable fraction
Calcium oxide	1305-78-8	-	2 1	-	- 4	Respirable fraction
Calcium silicate inhalable dust respirable	1344-95-2	- -	10 4	- -	- -	
Captan (ISO)	133-06-2	-	5	-	15	
Carbon black	1333-86-4	-	3.5	-	7	
Carbon dioxide	124-38-9	5000	9150	15000	27400	
Carbon disulphide	75-15-0	5	15	-	-	Sk
Carbon monoxide	630-08-0	20 30	23 35	100 200	117 232	BMGV Limits applicable to underground mining & tunnelling industries ONLY until 21/8/23
Carbon tetrachloride	56-23-5	1	6.4	5	32	Sk
Cellulose inhalable dust respirable	9004-34-6	- -	10 4	- -	20 -	
Chlorine	7782-50-5	-	-	0.5	1.5	
Chlorine dioxide	10049-04-4	0.1	0.28	0.3	0.84	
Chloroacetaldehyde	107-20-0	-	-	1	3.3	
2-Chloroacetophenone	532-27-4	0.05	0.32	-	-	
Chlorobenzene	108-90-7	1	4.7	3	14	Sk
Chlorodifluoromethane	75-45-6	1000	3590	-	-	
Chloroethane	75-00-3	50	134	-	-	
2-Chloroethanol	107-07-3	-	-	1	3.4	Sk
1-Chloro-2,3epoxypropane (Epichlorohydrin)	106-89-8	0.5	1.9	1.5	5.8	Carc
Chloroform	67-66-3	2	9.9	-	-	Sk
Chloromethane	74-87-3	50	105	100	210	
1-Chloro-4-nitrobenzene	100-00-5	-	1	-	2	Sk
Chlorosulphonic acid	7790-94-5	-	1	-	-	
Chlorpyrifos (ISO)	2921-88-2	-	0.2	-	0.6	Sk
Chromium	7440-47-3	-	0.5	-	-	
Chromium (II) compounds (as Cr)		-	0.5	-	-	
Chromium (III) compounds (as Cr)		-	0.5	-	-	
Chromium (VI) compounds (as Cr)		-	0.01 0.025 (process generated)$_1$	-	-	Carc, sen, BMGV

1 'Process generated' refers to exposures to Chromium (VI) Compounds generated as a result of a work process, such as fumes from welding.

Substance	CAS number	Workplace exposure limit				Comments
		Long-term exposure limit (8-hr TWA reference period)		Short-term exposure limit (15-minute reference period)		The Carc, Sen and Sk notations are not exhaustive.
		ppm	mg.m⁻³	ppm	mg.m⁻³	
Cobalt and Cobalt compounds (as Co)		-	0.1	-	-	Carc (cobalt dichloride and sulphate), Sen
Copper fume (as Cu)	7440-50-8	-	0.2	-	-	
Copper and compounds: dust and mists (as Cu)		-	1	-	2	
Cotton dust	(see paras 17-19)	-	2.5	-	-	
Cryofluorane (INN)	76-14-2	1000	7110	1250	8890	
Cumene	98-82-8	25	125	50	250	Sk
Cyanamide	420-04-2	0.58	1	-	-	Sk
Cyanides, except HCN, cyanogen and cyanogen chloride (as Cn)		-	5	-	-	Sk
Cyanogen chloride	506-77-4	-	-	0.3	0.77	
Cyclohexane	110-82-7	100	350	300	1050	
Cyclohexanol	108-93-0	50	208	-	-	
Cyclohexanone	108-94-1	10	41	20	82	Sk, BMGV
Cyclohexylamine	108-91-8	10	41	-	-	
2,4-D (ISO)	94-75-7	-	10	-	20	
Diacetyl	431-03-8	0.02	0.07	0.1	0.36	
Dialkyl 79 phthalate	83968-18-7	-	5	-	-	
Diallyl phthalate	131-17-9	-	5	-	-	
Diatomaceous earth, natural, respirable dust	61790-53-2	-	1.2	-	-	
Dibenzoyl peroxide	94-36-0	-	5	-	-	
Dibismuth tritelluride	1304-82-1	-	10	-	20	
Diboron trioxide	1303-86-2	-	10	-	20	
1,2-Dibromoethane (Ethylene dibromide)	106-93-4	0.5	3.9	-	-	Carc, Sk
Dibutyl hydrogen phosphate	107-66-4	1	8.7	2	17	
Dibutyl phthalate	84-74-2	-	5	-	10	
Dichloroacetylene	7572-29-4	-	-	0.1	0.39	
1,2-Dichlorobenzene (ortho-dichlorobenzene)	95-50-1	25	153	50	306	Sk
1,4 Dichlorobenzene (para-dichlorobenzene)	106-46-7	2	12	10	60	Sk
1,3-Dichloro-5,5-dimethylhydantoin	118-52-5	-	0.2	-	0.4	
1,1-Dichloroethane	75-34-3	100	-	-	-	Sk
1,2-Dichloroethane (Ethylene dichloride)	107-06-2	5	21	-	-	Carc, Sk
1,2-Dichloroethylene, cis:trans isomers 60:40	540-59-0	200	806	250	1010	
Dichlorofluoromethane	75-43-4	10	43	-	-	
Dichloromethane	75-09-2	100	353	200	706	BMGV, Sk
2,2'-Dichloro-4,4'methylene dianiline (MbOCA)	101-14-4	-	0.005	-	-	Carc, Sk, BMGV
Dicyclohexyl phthalate	84-61-7	-	5	-	-	
Dicyclopentadiene	77-73-6	5	27	-	-	
Diethylamine	109-89-7	5	15	10	30	

Substance	CAS number	Workplace exposure limit				Comments
		Long-term exposure limit (8-hr TWA reference period)		Short-term exposure limit (15-minute reference period)		The Carc, Sen and Sk notations are not exhaustive.
		ppm	mg.m⁻³	ppm	mg.m⁻³	
Diethyl ether	60-29-7	100	310	200	620	
Diethyl phthalate	84-66-2	-	5	-	10	
Diethyl sulphate	64-67-5	0.05	0.32	-	-	Carc, Sk
Dihydrogen selenide (as Se)	7783-07-5	0.02	0.07	0.05	0.17	
Diisobutyl phthalate	84-69-5	-	5	-	-	
Diisodecyl phthalate	26761-40-0	-	5	-	-	
Diisononyl phthalate	28553-12-0	-	5	-	-	
Diisooctyl phthalate	27554-26-3	-	5	-	-	
Diisopropylamine	108-18-9	5	21	-	-	
Diisopropyl ether	108-20-3	250	1060	310	1310	
N,N-Dimethylacetamide	127-19-5	10	36	20	72	Sk, BMGV
N,N-Dimethylaniline	121-69-7	5	25	10	50	Sk
N,N-Dimethylethylamine	598-56-1	10	30	15	46	
Dimethoxymethane	109-87-5	1000	3160	1250	3950	
Dimethylamine	124-40-3	2	3.8	6	11	
2-Dimethylaminoethanol	108-01-0	2	7.4	6	22	
Dimethyl ether	115-10-6	400	766	500	958	
N,N-Dimethylformamide	68-12-2	5	15	10	30	Sk
2,6-Dimethylheptan-4-one	108-83-8	25	148	-	-	
Dimethyl phthalate	131-11-3	-	5	-	10	
Dimethyl sulphate	77-78-1	0.05	0.26	-	-	Carc, Sk
Dinitrobenzene, all isomers	25154-54-5	0.15	1	0.5	3.5	Sk
Dinonyl phthalate	84-76-4	-	5	-	-	
1,4-Dioxane	123-91-1	20	73	-	-	Sk
Diphenylamine	122-39-4	-	10	-	20	
Diphenyl ether	101-84-8	1	7	2	14	
Diphosphorus pentasulphide	1314-80-3	-	1	-	2	
Disphosphorus pentoxide	1314-56-3	-	1	-	2	
Diquat dibromide (ISO)	85-00-7	-	0.5	-	1	
Disodium disulphite	7681-57-4	-	5	-	-	
Disodium tetraborate, anhydrous	1330-43-4	-	1	-	-	
Disodium tetraborate, decahydrate	1330-96-4	-	5	-	-	
Disodium tetraborate, pentahydrate	11130-12-4	-	1	-	-	
Disulphur dichloride	10025-67-9	-	-	1	5.6	
2,6-Di-*tert*-butyl-*p*-cresol	128-37-0	-	10	-	-	
6,6'-Di-*tert*-butyl-4,4'thiodi-*m*-cresol	96-69-5	-	10	-	20	
Diuron (ISO)	330-54-1	-	10	-	-	
Emery inhalable dust respirable	1302-74-5	- -	10 4	- -	- -	
Endosulfan (ISO)	115-29-7	-	0.1	-	0.3	Sk
Enflurane	13838-16-9	50	383	-	-	
Ethane-1,2-diol particulate vapour	107-21-1	- 20	10 52	- 40	- 104	Sk
Ethanethiol	75-08-1	0.5	1.3	2	5.2	
Ethanol	64-17-5	1000	1920	-	-	

Substance	CAS number	Workplace exposure limit				Comments
		Long-term exposure limit (8-hr TWA reference period)		Short-term exposure limit (15-minute reference period)		The Carc, Sen and Sk notations are not exhaustive.
		ppm	mg.m^{-3}	ppm	mg.m^{-3}	
2-Ethoxyethanol	110-80-5	2	8	-	-	Sk
2-Ethoxyethyl acetate	111-15-9	2	11	-	-	Sk
2-ethylhexan-1-ol	104-76-7	1	5.4	-	-	
2-Ethylhexyl chloroformate	24468-13-1	1	8	-	-	
Ethyl acetate	141-78-6	200	734	400	1468	
Ethyl acrylate	140-88-5	5	21	10	42	
Ethylamine	75-04-7	2	3.8	6	11	
Ethylbenzene	100-41-4	100	441	125	552	Sk
Ethyl chloroformate	541-41-3	1	4.5	-	-	
Ethyl cyanoacrylate	7085-85-0	-	-	0.3	1.5	
Ethyl formate	109-94-4	100	308	150	462	
Ethylene oxide	75-21-8	1	1.8	-	-	Carc, Sk
4-Ethylmorpholine	100-74-3	5	24	20	96	Sk
Ferrous foundry particulate inhalable dust respirable dust	See paras 20-22	- -	10 4	- -	- -	
Flour dust	See para 23	-	10	-	30	Sen
Fluoride (inorganic as F)	16984-48-8	-	2.5	-	-	
Fluorine	7782-41-4	1	1.6	1	1.6	
Formaldehyde	50-00-0	2	2.5	2	2.5	Carc
Formamide	75-12-7	20	37	30	56	
Formic acid	64-18-6	5	9.6	-	-	
2-Furaldehyde (furfural)	98-01-1	2	8	5	20	Sk
Germane	7782-65-2	0.2	0.64	0.6	1.9	
Glutaraldehyde	111-30-8	0.05	0.2	0.05	0.2	Sen
Glycerol, mist	56-81-5	-	10	-	-	
Glycerol trinitrate	55-63-0	0.01	0.095	0.02	0.19	Sk
Grain dust	See para 24	-	10	-	-	Sen
Graphite inhalable dust respirable	7440-44-0	- -	10 4	- -	- -	
Gypsum inhalable dust respirable	10101-41-4	- -	10 4	- -	- -	
Halogeno-platinum compounds (complex co-ordination compounds in which the platinum atom is directly co-ordinated to halide groups) (as Pt)	See paras 25-26	-	0.002	-	-	Sen
Halothane	151-67-7	10	82	-	-	
Hardwood dust (inhalable fraction)	See paras 40-41	-	3	-	-	Carc, Sen, If hardwood dusts are mixed with other wood dusts, the WEL shall apply to all the wood dusts present in that mixture.
n-Heptane	142-82-5	500	2085	-	-	
Heptan-2-one	110-43-0	50	237	100	475	Sk
Heptan-3-one	106-35-4	35	166	100	475	Sk
n-Hexane	110-54-3	20	72	-	-	

Substance	CAS number	Workplace exposure limit				Comments
		Long-term exposure limit (8-hr TWA reference period)		Short-term exposure limit (15-minute reference period)		The Carc, Sen and Sk notations are not exhaustive.
		ppm	mg.m^{-3}	ppm	mg.m^{-3}	
1,6-Hexanolactam dust only dust and vapour	105-60-2	- -	1 10	- -	3 20	
Hexan-2-one	591-78-6	5	21	-	-	Sk
Hydrazine	302-01-2	0.01	0.013	0.1	0.13	Carc, Sk
Hydrogen bromide	10035-10-6	-	-	3	10	
Hydrogen chloride (gas and aerosol mists)	7647-01-0	1	2	5	8	
Hydrogen cyanide	74-90-8	0.9	1	4.5	5	Sk
Hydrogen fluoride (as F)	7664-39-3	1.8	1.5	3	2.5	
Hydrogen peroxide	7722-84-1	1	1.4	2	2.8	
Hydrogen sulphide	7783-06-4	5	7	10	14	
Hydroquinone	123-31-9	-	0.5	-	-	
4-Hydroxy-4methylpentan-2-one	123-42-2	50	241	75	362	
2-Hydroxypropyl acrylate	999-61-1	0.5	2.7	-	-	Sk
2,2'-Iminodi(ethylamine)	111-40-0	1	4.3	-	-	Sk
Indene	95-13-6	10	48	15	72	
Indium and compounds (as In)		-	0.1	0	0.3	
Iodine	7553-56-2	-	-	0.1	1.1	
Iodoform	75-47-8	0.6	9.8	1	16	
Iodomethane	74-88-4	2	12	-	-	Sk
Iron oxide, fume (as Fe)	1309-37-1	-	5	-	10	
Iron salts (as Fe)		-	1	-	2	
Isobutyl acetate	110-19-0	150	724	187	903	
Isocyanates, all (as –NCO) Except methyl isocyanate		- -	0.02	- -	0.07	Sen
Isoflurane	26675-46-7	50	383	-	-	
Isoocytl alcohol (mixed isomers)	26952-21-6	50	271	-	-	
Isopentane	78-78-4	600	1800	-	-	
Isopropyl acetate	108-21-4	-	-	200	849	
Isopropyl chloroformate	108-23-6	1	5.1	-	-	
Kaolin, respirable dust	1332-58-7	-	2	-	-	
Ketene	463-51-4	0.5	0.87	1.5	2.6	
Limestone total inhalable respirable	1317-65-3	- -	10 4	- -	- -	
Liquefied petroleum gas	68476-85-7	1000	1750	1250	2180	Carc (only applies if LPG contains more than 0.1% of buta-1,3-diene)
Lithium hydride	7580-67-8	-	-	-	0.02	
Lithium hydroxide	1310-65-2	-	-	-	1	
Magnesite inhalable dust respirable dust	546-93-0	- -	10 4	- -	- -	
Magnesium oxide (as Mg) inhalable dust fume respirable dust	1309-48-4	- -	10 4	- -	- -	
Malathion (ISO)	121-75-5	-	10	-	-	Sk

Substance	CAS number	Workplace exposure limit				Comments
		Long-term exposure limit (8-hr TWA reference period)		Short-term exposure limit (15-minute reference period)		The Carc, Sen and Sk notations are not exhaustive.
		ppm	mg.m⁻³	ppm	mg.m⁻³	
Maleic anhydride	108-31-6	-	1	-	3	Sen
Manganese and its inorganic compounds (as Mn)		-	0.2 0.05	-	-	Inhalable fraction Respirable fraction
Marble total inhalable respirable	1317-65-3	- -	10 4	- -	- -	
Mercaptoacetic acid	68-11-1	1	3.8	-	-	
Mercury and divalent inorganic compounds including mercuric oxide and mercuric chloride (measured as mercury)		-	0.02	-	-	
Methacrylic acid	79-41-4	20	72	40	143	
Methacrylonitrile	126-98-7	1	2.8	-	-	Sk
Methanethiol	74-93-1	0.5	1.0	-	-	
Methanol	67-56-1	200	266	250	333	Sk
2-Methoxyethanol	109-86-4	1	3	-	-	Sk
2-(2-Methoxyethoxy) ethanol	111-77-3	10	50.1	-	-	Sk
2-Methoxyethyl acetate	110-49-6	1	5	-	-	Sk
(2-methoxymethylethoxy) propanol	34590-94-8	50	308	-	-	Sk
1-Methoxypropan-2-ol	107-98-2	100	375	150	560	Sk
1-Methoxypropyl acetate	108-65-6	50	274	100	548	Sk
Methyl acetate	79-20-9	200	616	250	770	
Methyl acrylate	96-33-3	5	18	10	36	
3-Methylbutan-1-ol	123-51-3	100	366	125	458	
Methyl cyanoacrylate	137-05-3	-	-	0.3	1.4	
Methyl formate	107-31-3	50	125	100	250	Sk
4,4'-Methylenedianiline	101-77-9	0.01	0.08	-	-	Carc, Sk, BMGV
Methyl ethyl ketone peroxides (MEKP)	1338-23-4	-	-	0.2	1.5	
Methyl methacrylate	80-62-6	50	208	100	416	
2-Methylcyclohexanone	583-60-8	50	233	75	350	
Methylcyclohexanol	25639-42-3	50	237	75	356	
Methyl isocyanate (as –NCO)	624-83-9	-	-	0.02	-	Sen
N-Methylaniline	100-61-8	0.5	2.2	-	-	Sk
n-Methyl-2-pyrrolidone	872-50-4	10	40	20	80	Sk
5-Methylheptan-3-one	541-85-5	10	53	20	107	
5-Methylhexan-2-one	110-12-3	20	95	100	475	Sk
2-Methylpentane-2,4-diol	107-41-5	25	123	25	123	
4-Methylpentan-2-ol	108-11-2	25	106	40	170	Sk
4-Methylpentan-2-one	108-10-1	50	208	100	416	Sk, BMGV
2-Methylpropan-1-ol	78-83-1	50	154	75	231	
2-Methylpropan-2-ol	75-65-0	100	308	150	462	
Methyl-tert-butyl-ether	1634-04-4	50	183.5	100	367	
Mica total inhalable respirable	12001-26-2	- -	10 0.8	- -	- -	
MMMF (Machine-made mineral fibre) (except for refractory ceramic fibres and special purpose fibres)		5mg. m⁻³ and 2 fibres/ millilitre	-	-	-	

Substance	CAS number	Workplace exposure limit				Comments
		Long-term exposure limit (8-hr TWA reference period)		Short-term exposure limit (15-minute reference period)		The Carc, Sen and Sk notations are not exhaustive.
		ppm	mg.m^{-3}	ppm	mg.m^{-3}	
Molybdenum compounds (as Mo) soluble compounds insoluble compounds		- -	5 10	- -	10 20	
Monochloroacetic acid	79-11-8	0.3	1.2	-	-	Sk
Morpholine	110-91-8	10	36	20	72	Sk
Neopentane	463-82-1	600	1800	-	-	
Nickel and its inorganic compounds (except nickel tetracarbonyl): water-soluble nickel compounds (as Ni) nickel and water-insoluble nickel compounds (as Ni)		- -	0.1 0.5	- -	- -	Sk, Carc (nickel oxides and sulphides) Sen (nickel sulphate)
Nicotine	54-11-5	-	0.5	-	1.5	Sk
Nitric acid	7697-37-2	-	-	1	2.6	
Nitrobenzene	98-95-3	0.2	1	-	-	Sk
Nitroethane	79-24-3	20	62	100	312	Sk
Nitrogen dioxide*	10102-44-0	0.5	0.96	1	1.91	Does not apply to underground mining and tunnelling industries until 21/8/23
Nitrogen monoxide*	10102-43-9	2 25	2.5 30	- -	- -	Limit applicable to underground mining & tunnelling industries ONLY until 21/8/23
Nitromethane	75-52-5	100	254	150	381	
2-Nitropropane	79-46-9	5	18	-	-	Carc
Nitrous oxide	10024-97-2	100	183	-	-	
Orthophosphoric acid	7664-38-2	-	1	-	2	
Osmium tetraoxide (as Os)	20816-12-0	0.0002	0.002	0.0006	0.006	
Oxalic acid	144-62-7	-	1	-	2	
2,2'-Oxydiethanol	111-46-6	23	101	-	-	
Ozone	10028-15-6	-	-	0.2	0.4	
Paracetamol, inhalable dust	103-90-2	-	10	-	-	
Paraffin wax, fume	8002-74-2	-	2	-	6	
Paraquat dichloride (ISO), respirable dust	1910-42-5	-	0.08	-	-	
Pentacarbonyliron (as Fe)	13463-40-6	0.01	0.08	-	-	
Pentaerythritol inhalable dust respirable dust	115-77-5	- -	10 4	- -	20 -	
Pentan-2-one	107-87-9	200	716	250	895	
Pentan-3-one	96-22-0	200	716	250	895	
Pentane	109-66-0	600	1800	-	-	
Pentyl acetates (all isomers)		50	270	100	541	
2-Phenylpropene	98-83-9	50	246	100	491	
Phenol	108-95-2	2	7.8	4	16	Sk
p-Phenylenediamine	106-50-3	-	0.1	-	-	Sk
Phorate (ISO)	298-02-2	-	0.05	-	0.2	Sk
Phosgene	75-44-5	0.02	0.08	0.06	0.25	

Substance	CAS number	Workplace exposure limit				Comments
		Long-term exposure limit (8-hr TWA reference period)		Short-term exposure limit (15-minute reference period)		The Carc, Sen and Sk notations are not exhaustive.
		ppm	mg.m⁻³	ppm	mg.m⁻³	
Phosphine	7803-51-2	0.1	0.14	0.2	0.28	
Phosphorus pentachloride	10026-13-8	0.1	0.87	0.2	2	
Phosphorus trichloride	7719-12-2	0.2	1.1	0.5	2.9	
Phosphorus, yellow	7723-14-0	-	0.1	-	0.3	
Phosphoryl trichloride	10025-87-3	0.2	1.3	0.6	3.8	
Phthalic anhydride	85-44-9	-	4	-	12	Sen
Picloram (ISO)	1918-02-1	-	10	-	20	
Picric acid	88-89-1	-	0.1	-	0.3	
Piperazine	110-85-0	-	0.1	-	0.3	Sen
Piperazine dihydrochloride	142-64-3	-	0.1	-	0.3	Sen
Piperidine	110-89-4	1	3.5	-	-	Sk
Plaster of Paris inhalable dust respirable dust	26499-65-0	- -	10 4	- -	- -	
Platinum compounds, soluble (except certain halogeno-Pt compounds) (as Pt)		-	0.002	-	-	
Platinum metal	7440-06-4	-	5	-	-	
Polychlorinated biphenyls (PCB)	1336-36-3	-	0.1	-	-	Sk
Polyvinyl chlorid inhalable dust respirable dust	9002-86-2	- -	10 4	- -	- -	
Portland cement inhalable dust respirable dust	65997-15-1	- -	10 4	- -	- -	
Potassium cyanide (as cyanide)	151-50-8		1		5	Sk
Potassium hydroxide	1310-58-3	-	-	-	2	
Propane-1,2-diol total vapour and particulates particulates	57-55-6	150 -	474 10	- -	- -	
Propan-1-ol	71-23-8	200	500	250	625	Sk
Propan-2-ol	67-63-0	400	999	500	1250	
Propionic acid	79-09-4	10	31	15	46	
Propoxur (ISO)	114-26-1	-	0.5	-	2	
Propranolol	525-66-6	-	2	-	6	
n-Propyl acetate	109-60-4	200	849	250	1060	
Propylene oxide	75-56-9	1	2.4	-	-	Carc
Prop-2-yn-1-ol	107-19-7	1	2.3	3	7	Sk
Pulverised fuel ash inhalable dust respirable dust		- -	10 4	- -	- -	
Pyrethrum (purified of sensitising lactones)	8003-34-7	-	1	-	-	
Pyridine	110-86-1	5	16	10	33	
2-Pyridylamine	504-29-0	0.5	2	2	7.8	
Pyrocatechol	102-80-9	5	23	-	-	
Refractory ceramic fibres and special purpose fibres - total inhalable dust - respirable fraction		5mg/m3 0.3 fibre/millilitre		-	-	Carc

Substance	CAS number	Workplace exposure limit				Comments
		Long-term exposure limit (8-hr TWA reference period)		Short-term exposure limit (15-minute reference period)		The Carc, Sen and Sk notations are not exhaustive.
		ppm	mg.m^{-3}	ppm	mg.m^{-3}	
Resorcinol	108-46-3	10	46	20	92	Sk
Rhodium (as Rh) metal fume and dust soluble salts		- -	0.1 0.001	- -	0.3 0.003	
Rosin-based solder flux fume	8050-09-7	-	0.05	-	0.15	Sen
Rotenone (ISO)	83-79-4	-	5	-	10	
Rouge total inhalable respirable	1309-37-1	- -	10 4	- -	- -	
Rubber fume	See paras 31–36	-	0.6	-	-	Carc, limit relates to cyclohexane soluble material
Rubber process dust	See paras 31–36	-	6	-	-	Carc
Selenium and compounds, except hydrogen selenide (as Se)		-	0.1	-	-	
Silane	7803-62-5	0.5	0.67	1	1.3	
Silica, amorphous inhalable dust respirable dust		- -	6 2.4	- -	- -	
Silica, respirable crystalline (respirable fraction)		-	0.1	-	-	Carc (where generated as a result of a work process)
Silica, fused respirable dust	60676-86-0	-	0.08	-	-	
Silicon inhalable dust respirable dust	7440-21-3	- -	10 4	- -	- -	
Silicon carbide (not whiskers) total inhalable respirable	409-21-2	- -	10 4	- -	- -	
Silver (soluble compounds as Ag)		-	0.01	-	-	
Silver, metallic	7440-22-4	-	0.1	-	-	
Sodium azide (as NaN$_3$)	26628-22-8	-	0.1	-	0.3	Sk
Sodium 2-(2,4-dichlorophenoxy) ethyl sulphate	136-78-7	-	10	-	20	
Sodium cyanide (as cyanide)	143-33-9	-	1	-	5	Sk
Sodium hydrogen sulphite	7631-90-5	-	5	-	-	
Sodium hydroxide	1310-73-2	-	-	-	2	
Softwood dust	See paras 40-41	-	5	-	-	Sen, If softwood dusts are mixed with hardwood dusts, the WEL for hardwood dusts shall apply to all the wood dusts present in that mixture.
Starch total inhalable respirable	9005-25-8	- -	10 4	- -	- -	
Styrene	100-42-5	100	430	250	1080	
Subtilisins	1395-21-7 (*Bacillus subtilis* BPN) 9014-01-1 (*Bacillus subtilis* Carlsberg)	-	0.00004	-	-	Sen
Sucrose	57-50-1	-	10	-	20	

Substance	CAS number	Workplace exposure limit				Comments
		Long-term exposure limit (8-hr TWA reference period)		Short-term exposure limit (15-minute reference period)		The Carc, Sen and Sk notations are not exhaustive.
		ppm	mg.m⁻³	ppm	mg.m⁻³	
Sulfotep (ISO)	3689-24-5	-	0.1	-	-	Sk
Sulphur dioxide	7446-09-5	0.5	1.3	1	2.7	
Sulphur hexafluoride	2551-62-4	1000	6070	1250	7590	
Sulphuric acid (mist)	7664-93-9	-	0.05	-	-	The mist is defined as the thoracic fraction
Sulphuryl difluoride	2699-79-8	5	21	10	42	
Talc, respirable dust	14807-96-6	-	1	-	-	
Tantalum	7440-25-7	-	5	-	10	
Tellurium and compounds, except hydrogen telluride (as Te)		-	0.1	-	-	
Terphenyls, all isomers	26140-60-3	-	-	0.5	4.8	
Terphenyl, hydrogenated	61788-32-7	2	19	5	48	
1,1,2,2-Tetrabromoethane	79-27-6	0.5	7.2	-	-	Sk
Tertiary-butyl-methylether	1634-04-4	50	183.5	100	367	
Tetracarbonylnickel (as Ni)	13463-39-3	-	-	0.1	0.24	
Tetrachloroethylene	127-18-4	20	138	40	275	Sk
Tetraethyl orthosilicate	78-10-4	5	44	-	-	
1,1,1,2-Tetrafluoroethane (HFC 134a)	811-97-2	1000	4240	-	-	
Tetrahydrofuran	109-99-9	50	150	100	300	Sk
Tetrasodium pyrophosphate	7722-88-5	-	5	-	-	
Thallium, soluble compounds (as Tl)		-	0.1	-	-	Sk
Thionyl chloride	7719-09-7	-	-	1	4.9	
Tin compounds, inorganic except SnH₄, (as Sn)		-	2	-	4	
Tin compounds, organic, except Cyhexatin (ISO), (as Sn)		-	0.1	-	0.2	Sk
Titanium dioxide total inhalable respirable	13463-67-7	- -	10 4	- -	- -	
Toluene	108-88-3	50	191	100	384	Sk
p-Toluenesulphonyl chloride	98-59-9	-	-	-	5	
o-Toluidine	95-53-4	0.1	0.5	-	-	Carc, Sk
Tributyl phosphate, all isomers	126-73-8	-	5	-	5	
1,2,4-Trichlorobenzene	120-82-1	1	-	5	-	Sk
1,1,1-Trichloroethane	71-55-6	100	555	200	1110	
Trichloroethylene	79-01-6	100	550	150	820	Carc, Sk
Trichloronitromethane	76-06-2	0.1	0.68	0.3	2.1	
Triethylamine	121-44-8	2	8	4	17	Sk
Triglycidyl isocyanurate (TGIC)	2451-62-9	-	0.1	-	-	Carc
Trimellitic anhydride	552-30-7	-	0.04	-	0.12	Sen
Trimethylbenzenes, all isomers or mixtures	25551-13-7	25	125	-	-	
3,5,5-trimethylcyclohex-2enone	78-59-1	-	-	5	29	
Trimethyl phosphite	121-45-9	2	10	-	-	
2,4,6-Trinitrotoluene	118-96-7	-	0.5	-	-	Sk
Tri-o-tolyl phosphate	78-30-8	-	0.1	-	0.3	
Triphenyl phosphate	115-86-6	-	3	-	6	

Substance	CAS number	Workplace exposure limit				Comments
		Long-term exposure limit (8-hr TWA reference period)		Short-term exposure limit (15-minute reference period)		The Carc, Sen and Sk notations are not exhaustive.
		ppm	mg.m^{-3}	ppm	mg.m^{-3}	
Tungsten and compounds (as W) soluble compounds insoluble compounds and others	7440-33-7	- -	1 5	- -	3 10	
Turpentine	8006-64-2	100	566	150	850	
Vanadium pentoxide	1314-62-1	-	0.05	-	-	
Vinyl acetate	108-05-4	5	17.6	10	35.2	
Vinyl chloride	75-01-4	1	2.6	-	-	Carc
Vinylidene chloride	75-35-4	2	8	5	20	
Wool process dust	See para 42	-	10	-	-	
Xylene, o-,m-,p- or mixed isomers	1330-20-7	50	220	100	441	Sk, BMGV
Yttrium	7440-65-5	-	1	-	3	
Zinc chloride, fume	7646-85-7	-	1	-	2	
Zinc distearate inhalable dust respirable dust	557-05-1	- -	10 4	- -	20 -	
Zirconium compounds (as Zr)		-	5	-	10	

SUPPLEMENTARY INFORMATION FOR TABLE 1

Definitions

Cotton dust

17   Cotton is the cellulose fibre that grows inside the seed pods (or bolls) of the cotton plant. When mature, the boll breaks and the cotton appears as a soft wad of fine fibres. After picking, the cotton is separated from the seed etc, and is packed and compressed into bales.

18   The WEL, which is based on personal sampling, applies to exposure to inhalable dust during the handling of raw and waste cotton including blends containing raw or waste cotton, with the following exceptions:

- dust from weaving, knitting, braiding and subsequent processes;
- dust from bleached or dyed cotton; and
- dust from finished articles, eg garments.

   (Where the WEL does not apply, exposure should still be adequately controlled.)

19   MDHS14/4[4] gives information about air sampling for comparison with the WEL. The sampler should be an Institute of Occupational Medicine (IOM) inhalable dust sampler or any other sampler giving equivalent results.

Ferrous foundry particulate

20   The atmospheric contamination in ferrous (iron and steel) foundries is a complex mixture of dust, fume, gases and vapours produced as a consequence of the foundry processes. The particulate fraction of the atmospheric contamination is described as ferrous foundry particulate (FFP). The composition of FFP will vary according to the process producing it and the materials used.

21   During the making of cores and moulds, vapours and gases from the binder system may be given off, and particles of sand, including respirable silica (possibly coated with unreacted or reacted binder materials) can become airborne. When molten metal is poured into the moulds, decomposition products can be produced from organic binders and additives in the mould. The decomposition products may bind to particles of sand or metal oxide. At knockout and shakeout, sand particles (which may be coated with thermally degraded binder material) are the main contaminants produced. Metal finishing operations can give rise to fume as well as airborne metal, metal oxide particles and coated sand particles.

22   Some of the individual components of the atmospheric contamination are known to be carcinogenic or mutagenic and some have been assigned WELs. The interrelationship between the components of FFP is complex and it is inappropriate to rely on the individual WELs in assessing overall exposure to airborne contaminants in the foundry atmosphere. Airborne particulate is considered to be a suitable surrogate for overall exposure assessment in ferrous foundries. FFP is measured as total inhalable particulate (TIP) and respirable particulate (RP). Where identified components of the contamination have WELs, these limits will apply.

Flour dust

23 Flour dust is taken to be finely ground particles of cereals or pulses (including contaminants) that result from any grinding process and from any subsequent handling and use of that 'flour'. Any additives (eg flour improvers) are included in this definition only after they have been added to the final product mix.

Grain dust

24 Grain dust is taken to be dust arising from the harvesting, drying, handling, storage or processing of barley, wheat, oats, maize and rye, including contaminants.

Halogeno-platinum compounds

25 These are co-ordination compounds in which a platinum atom or ion is directly co-ordinated to one or more halide (ie fluoride, chloride, bromide or iodide) ions. These compounds are subject to a WEL and have a Sen notation. These substances are listed in section C of *Asthmagen? Critical assessments of the evidence for agents implicated in occupational asthma.*[5]

26 For substances which, although they contain platinum and halide ions, the halogen is not directly co-coordinated by a chemical bond to the platinum, the WEL for soluble platinum compounds is applicable.

Machine-made mineral fibres (MMMF)

27 Machine-made (formerly 'man-made') mineral fibres are defined as man-made vitreous (silicate) fibres with random orientation with alkaline oxide and alkali earth oxide ($Na_2O+K_2O+CaO+MgO+BaO$) content greater than 18% by weight. Neither the gravimetric limit nor the fibres in air limits should be exceeded. Fibre concentrations of MMMFs must be measured or calculated by a method approved by HSE.

28 A separate limit applies to other MMMFs which are not covered by this definition (see paragraph 30).

Pulverised fuel ash

29 Pulverised fuel ash (PFA), sometimes known as precipitation ash, is a fine grey fuel ash powder, composed mainly of alumino-silicate amorphous spheres. It is produced when pulverised coal is burnt in a coal-fired power station. It is collected and separated into various grades for use as a filler in civil engineering and land reclamation, in ready-mix concrete, as a grout in block/cementitious products and in the manufacture of other products used by the construction industry.

Refractory ceramic fibre (RCF)

30 RCFs are man-made vitreous (silicate) fibres with random orientation with alkaline oxide and alkali earth oxide ($Na_2O+K_2O+CaO+MgO+BaO$) content less or equal to 18% by weight. The term 'RCF' also includes non-oxide ceramic fibre such as boron and silicon carbides and nitrides. Fibre concentrations of RCF must be measured or calculated by a method approved by HSE.

Rubber fume and rubber process dust

31 Rubber fume is fume evolved in the mixing, milling and blending of natural rubber or synthetic elastomers, or of natural rubber and synthetic polymers combined with chemicals, and in the processes which convert the resultant blends into finished process dust products or parts thereof, and including any inspection procedures where fume continues to be evolved.

32   The limit relates to cyclohexane soluble material determined by the method described in MDHS47/3 *Determination of rubber process dust and rubber fume (measured as cyclohexane-soluble material) in air.*[6]

33   Rubber process dust is dust arising in the stages of rubber manufacture where ingredients are handled, weighed, added to or mixed with uncured material or synthetic elastomers. It does not include dusts arising from the abrasion of cured rubber.

34   Where the airborne material contains a mixture of substances, one or more of which is assigned a WEL, that limit will apply to the individual substance and at the same time the rubber process dust limit will apply to the mix dust as a whole. Where the airborne material is effectively a single substance with a WEL, that limit alone will apply.

35   Methods for personal sampling and measurement of inhalable dusts are available in MDHS14/4[4] and MDHS47/3.[6] As with the fume, the dust is determined gravimetrically but, unlike the fume, the dust determination does not involve solvent extraction.

36   **Note:** Dust produced by the abrasion of cured rubber should be dealt with as described in paragraphs 43–46, ie dust of any kind when present at a substantial concentration in air is covered by COSHH.

Subtilisins

37   Subtilisins are proteolytic enzymes derived from *Bacillus subtilis.* They are used in biological washing powders, animal feedstuffs etc. The enzyme preparation contains active enzyme, inactive enzyme and protein residues.

38   One of the suitable measurement methods is the fluorescence polarisation technique developed by the Health and Safety Laboratory (HSL). The previous limit for subtilisin was based on high-volume static sampling to achieve sufficient sensitivity. However, improvements in the analytical methodology have improved the sensitivity and the WEL for subtilisin reflects this. The limit is based on standard personal sampling (MDHS14/4).[4] Short-term reference period (15 minute) sampling is not appropriate.

Talc

39   Talc is defined as the mineral talc together with other hydrous phyllosilicates including chlorite and carbonate materials which occur with it, but excluding amphibole asbestos and crystalline silica.

Wood dust

40   Wood dust is a general term covering a wide variety of airborne wood dusts. Timbers have been divided into two different groups, namely hardwoods and softwoods. Hardwoods are timbers from deciduous trees, including trees from both temperate and tropical zones such as beech, ash, oak, mahogany and teak. Softwoods are mainly from coniferous trees such as Scots pine, yew and cedar.

41   Dust is generated by the machining and working of wood and wood-containing materials such as chipboard and fibreboard. Operations such as sawing, turning and routing produce relatively coarse dust, while sanding and assembly operations generate fine dust.

Wool process dust

42   Wool process dust is the term used to describe the dust generated in the production of woollen and worsted textiles. This includes all factory processes from the receipt of the raw wool up to the finished product (in the case of carpet manufacture) and up to, and including, weaving, knitting or non-woven cloth production. It does not cover agricultural processes, including any sorting or baling done on the farm. The term 'wool', in this case, refers to sheep's wool and wool blends only. It does

not include other speciality fibres – such as goat hair (including cashmere and mohair), camel hair or alpaca. Such fibres differ from wool in structure and it is not certain that the composition of the dust or the potential health risk is the same as with wool process dust.

Dust

43   The COSHH definition of a substance hazardous to health includes dust of any kind when present at a concentration in air equal to or greater than 10 mg.m^{-3} 8-hour TWA of inhalable dust or 4 mg.m^{-3} 8-hour TWA of respirable dust. This means that any dust will be subject to COSHH if people are exposed to dust above these levels. Some dusts have been assigned specific WELs and exposure to these must comply with the appropriate limits.

44   Most industrial dusts contain particles of a wide range of sizes. The behaviour, deposition and fate of any particular particle after entry into the human respiratory system, and the body response that it elicits, depend on the nature and size of the particle. HSE distinguishes two size fractions for limit-setting purposes termed 'inhalable' and 'respirable'.

45   Inhalable dust approximates to the fraction of airborne material that enters the nose and mouth during breathing and is therefore available for deposition in the respiratory tract. Respirable dust approximates to the fraction that penetrates to the gas exchange region of the lung. Fuller definitions and explanatory material are given in MDHS14/4.[4]

46   Where dusts contain components that have their own assigned WEL, all the relevant limits should be complied with.

Fume

47   The word 'fume' is often used to include gases and vapours. This is not the case for exposure limits where 'fume' should normally be applied to solid particles generated by chemical reactions or condensed from the gaseous state, usually after volatilisation from melted substances. The generation of fume is often accompanied by a chemical reaction such as oxidation or thermal breakdown.

Carcinogenic and mutagenic substances

48   Regulation 2 of COSHH defines a carcinogen as:

(a)   *A substance or mixture which meets the criteria for classification as a category 1A or 1B carcinogen set out in Annex I to the CLP Regulation [Classification, Labelling and Packaging of Chemicals Regulation EC 1272/2008] whether or not the substance or mixture would be required to be classified under the Regulation;* or

(b)   *a substance or mixture which is—*
(i)   referred to in Schedule 1 [of COSHH]; or
(ii)   released by a process referred to in Schedule 1 [of COSHH] and is a substance hazardous to health.

49   And defines a mutagen as:

A substance or mixture which meets the criteria for classification as a category 1A or 1B germ cell mutagen set out in Annex I to the CLP Regulation, whether or not the substance or mixture would be required to be classified under that Regulation.

50   These definitions also cover any substance or mixture that would be classified as a carcinogen or mutagen although not covered by CLP Regulation by virtue of that Regulation being disapplied i.e. medicines in the finished state intended for the final user. They also cover circumstances where there is no supply e.g. the movement of unpackaged substances and mixtures within a factory, and substances generated as a result of a work process.

51   Regulation 7(5) of COSHH sets out clear requirements for the control of exposure to carcinogenic and mutagenic substances. Also Regulation 7(7)(c) includes a requirement for exposure to be reduced to as low as is reasonably practicable for substances that are assigned the hazard statements H340 (may cause genetic defects), H350 (may cause cancer) or H350i (may cause cancer by inhalation) or which are listed in Schedule 1 of COSHH.

Asbestos and lead

52   Asbestos and lead are regulated separately; you can find more information on these substances on the HSE website www.hse.gov.uk.

Substances that can cause occupational asthma

53   Substances that can cause occupational asthma (also known as asthmagens and respiratory sensitisers) can induce a state of specific airway hyper-responsiveness via an immunological irritant or other mechanism. Once the airways have become hyper-responsive, further exposure to the substance, sometimes even in tiny quantities, may cause respiratory symptoms. These symptoms can range in severity from a runny nose to asthma. Not all workers who are exposed to a sensitiser will become hyper-responsive and it is impossible to identify in advance those who are likely to becomc hyper-responsive.

54   Substances that can cause occupational asthma should be distinguished from substances which may trigger the symptoms of asthma in people with pre-existing airway hyper-responsiveness, but which do not include the disease themselves. The latter substances are not classified as asthmagens or respiratory sensitisers. Further information can be found in the HSE publication *Asthmagen? Critical assessments of the evidence for agents implicated in occupational asthma.*[5]

55   Wherever it is reasonably practicable, exposure to substances that can cause occupational asthma should be prevented. Where this is not possible, the primary aim is to apply adequate standards of control to prevent workers from becoming hyper-responsive. For substances that can cause occupational asthma, COSHH requires that exposure be reduced to as low as is reasonably practicable. Activities giving rise to short-term peak concentrations should receive particular attention when risk management is being considered. Health surveillance is appropriate for all employees exposed or liable to be exposed to a substance which may cause occupational asthma and there should be appropriate consultation with an occupational health professional over the degree of risk and level of surveillance.

56   The 'Sen' notation in the list of WELs has been assigned only to those substances which may cause occupational asthma in the categories shown in Table 1. It should be remembered that other substances not in these tables may cause occupational asthma. HSE's asthma web pages (www.hse.gov.uk/asthma) provide further information.

Asphyxiants

57   Some gases and vapours, when present at high concentrations in air, act as simple asphyxiants by reducing the oxygen content by dilution to such an extent that life cannot be supported. Many asphyxiants are odourless and colourless and not readily detectable. Monitoring the oxygen content of the air is often the best means of ensuring safety. There are substantial risks if the concentration of oxygen in the atmosphere varies from normal (20.8%) under normal atmospheric pressure. With reference to specific statutory requirements, any difference in oxygen content from normal should be investigated, the risks assessed, and appropriate measures taken in

the light of the risk. In particular, the Mines Regulations 2014[7] (Regulation 43) refer to the duty upon the mine operator to secure ventilation below ground adequate for diluting gases and providing air containing sufficient oxygen. It also specifies the amount of oxygen in the general body of the air to be not less than 19% by volume.

58   Particular care is necessary when dense asphyxiants, eg argon, are used since very high, localised concentrations can arise due to their collecting in pits, confined spaces and other low-lying areas where ventilation is likely to be poor.

59   Many asphyxiants present a fire or explosion risk. The concentrations at which these risks can arise are liable to be well below those at which asphyxiation is likely to occur and should be taken into account when assessing the hazards.

Pesticides

60   Substances used as active ingredients in pesticides are listed under their systematic chemical names and/or their (ISO) common names. These may sometimes be used as parts of the names of proprietary pesticide formulations. In all cases, the exposure limit applies to the specific active ingredient in the workplace atmosphere and not the formulation as a whole.

Exposure in mines

61   The Mines Regulations 2014 [7] impose duties on mine operators to protect persons at work in coal mines from risks to their health arising from exposure to inhalable and respirable dust.

APPLYING OCCUPATIONAL EXPOSURE LIMITS

Scope of the limits

62   The list of WELs, unless otherwise stated, relates to personal exposure to substances hazardous to health in the air of the workplace. The limits cannot be adapted readily to evaluate or control non-occupational exposure, eg levels of contamination in the neighbourhood close to an industrial plant. WELs are approved only for application to people at work. Employers should also take into account their duties under the Environmental Protection Act.[8] WELs are approved only for use where the atmospheric pressure is between 900 and 1100 millibars. This covers the normal range of meterological variations in Great Britain and slightly pressurised workplaces such as clean rooms, but not the hyperbaric conditions which may be encountered in, for example, tunnelling or diving. To enable WELs to be applied in hyperbaric conditions, the limits should be expressed as a partial pressure or mass/volume concentration at higher pressures. This approach is discussed in detail in EH75/2 *Occupational exposure limits for hyperbaric conditions.*[9]

63   Workplace exposure limits as set out in regulation 7 of COSHH are intended to be used for normal working conditions in factories or other workplaces. Employers also have a clear responsibility to ensure that the plant is designed, operated and maintained in a way that avoids accidents and emergencies. Where appropriate, detection, alarm and response measures should be used to minimise the effect of any such unplanned events.

Long-term and short-term exposure limits

64   Effects of exposure to substances hazardous to health vary considerably depending on the nature of the substance and the pattern of exposure. Some effects require prolonged or accumulated exposure. **The long-term (8-hour TWA) exposure limit** is intended to control such effects by restricting the total intake by inhalation over one or more work shifts, depending on the length of the shift. Other effects may be seen after brief exposures. Short-term exposure limits (usually 15 minutes) may be applied to control these effects. For those substances for which no short-term limit is specified, it is recommended that a figure of three times the long-term limit be used as a guideline for controlling short-term peaks in exposure. Some workplace activities give rise to frequent short (less than 15 minutes) periods of high exposure which, if averaged over time, do not exceed either an 8-hour TWA or a 15-minute TWA. Such exposures have the potential to cause harm and should be subject to reasonably practicable means of control unless a 'suitable and sufficient' risk assessment shows no risk to health from such exposures.

65   In some situations such as in submarines and saturation diving, the occupational exposure is essentially continuous. In these cases, a continuous exposure limit should be derived by dividing the 8-hour TWA exposure limit by a factor of 5. Further information can be found in EH75/2.[9]

66   Both the long-term and short-term exposure limits are expressed as airborne concentrations averaged over a specified period of time. The period for the long-term limit is normally 8 hours; when a different period is used this is stated. The averaging period for the short-term exposure limit

is normally 15 minutes, such a limit applying to any 15-minute period throughout the working shift. Exposure to substances hazardous to health should be calculated according to the approved method, which is reproduced in the section 'Calculation methods'.

Units of measurement

67   In workplace exposure limits, concentrations of airborne particles (fume, dust etc) are usually expressed in mg.m^{-3}. In the case of dusts, the limits in Table 1 refer to the 'inhalable' fraction unless specifically indicated as referring to the 'respirable' fraction (see paragraphs 43-46). Exceptionally, the limits for MMMFs and for RCFs can be expressed either as mg.m^{-3} or as fibres per millilitre of air (fibres.ml^{-1}). WELs for volatile substances are usually expressed in both parts per million by volume (ppm) and milligrams per cubic metre (mg.m^{-3}). For these substances, limits are set in ppm, and a conversion to mg.m^{-3} is calculated. The value in mg.m^{-3} for a given concentration in ppm depends on the temperature and pressure of the ambient air, which in reality vary over time. Therefore, conversion calculations are based on a standard set of typical conditions.

Conversion and rounding of WELs expressed in ppm to mg.m^{-3}

68   The limits in Table 1 have been calculated from first principles, using the following method:

$$\text{WEL in mg.m}^{-3} = \frac{\text{WEL in ppm} \times \text{MWt}}{24.05526}$$

where MWt is the molecular weight (molar mass in g.mol^{-1}) of the substance.

Note that 24.05526 l.mol^{-1} is the molar volume of an ideal gas at 20°C and 1 atmosphere pressure (760 mm mercury, 101325 Pa, 1.01325 bar).

69   The results have been rounded using the following procedure:

Range containing the newly calculated WEL (in mg.m^{-3})	Round to:
Less than 0.1	1 significant figure
0.1 to less than 100	2 significant figures
100 or over	3 significant figures

Calculation of exposure

70   Exposure to substances hazardous to health should be calculated according to the approved method. The calculated exposure should then be compared with the workplace exposure limits for that substance for the purposes of determining compliance with COSHH, regulation 7. Where a WEL is listed for both a long-term reference period and a short-term reference period, it will be necessary to compare the calculated exposures with the appropriate WELs for both periods.

Limitations to the application of exposure limits

71   The exposure limits relate to personal monitoring.

Other factors

72 Working conditions which impose additional stress on the body, such as exposure to ultra-violet radiation and high temperatures, pressures and humidity, may increase the toxic response to a substance. In such cases, specialist advice may be necessary to evaluate the effects of these factors.

Absorption through the skin

73 For most substances, the main route of entry into the body is by inhalation and the exposure limits given in this guidance relate solely to exposure by this route. However, some substances have the ability to penetrate intact skin and become absorbed into the body, thus contributing to systemic toxicity.

74 Absorption through the skin can result from localised contamination, for example, from a splash on the skin or clothing, or in certain cases from exposure to high atmospheric concentrations of vapour. This may result in a substantial body burden so that serious effects may result with little or no warning. It is necessary to take special precautions to prevent skin contact when handling these substances. Where the 'Sk' notation has been assigned and the methods of use provide a potential exposure route via skin absorption, these factors should be taken into account in determining the adequacy of the control measures. Further guidance is given on the adequate control of exposure by routes other than inhalation in COSHH ACOP [2] and on the HSE website www.hse.gov.uk/skin which deals with skin at work.

CALCULATION METHODS

Calculation of exposure with regard to the specified reference periods

75   This section reproduces the approved methods for the calculation of exposure in relation to the 8-hour and short-term reference periods. **These methods are legally binding because they have been approved by the Health and Safety Commission.**

Notice of approval

The Health and Safety Commission has on 9 November 2004 approved the methods of calculation set out in the Schedule to this Notice for the purpose of determining exposure in relation to the reference periods for workplace exposure limits as specified in regulation 2(1) of the Control of Substances Hazardous to Health Regulations 2002 (as amended) and occupational exposure limit for lead as specified in regulation 2(1) of the Control of Lead at Work Regulations 2002.

Signed

SUSAN MAWER
Secretary to the Health and Safety Commission
9 November 2004

The Health and Safety Commission (HSC) and the Health and Safety Executive (HSE) merged on 1 April 2008 to form a single national regulatory body. From that date, the Health and Safety Executive became responsible for approving Codes of Practice, with the consent of the Secretary of State.

Schedule

Part 1 The 8-hour reference period

1   The term '8-hour reference period' relates to the procedure whereby the occupational exposures in any 24-hour period are treated as equivalent to a single uniform exposure for 8 hours (the 8-hour time-weighted average (TWA) exposure).

2   The 8-hour TWA may be represented mathematically by:

$$\frac{C_1T_1 + C_2T_2 + \ldots C_nT_n}{8}$$

where C_1 is the occupational exposure and T_1 is the associated exposure time in hours in any 24-hour period.

Example 1

3   The operator works for 7 hours 20 minutes on a process in which he is exposed to a substance hazardous to health. The average exposure during that period is measured as 0.12 mg.m⁻³.

The 8-hour TWA =

7 h 20 min (7.33 h) at 0.12 mg.m⁻³

40 min (0.67 h) at 0 mg.m⁻³

That is

$$\frac{(0.12 \times 7.33) + (0 \times 0.67)}{8}$$

= 0.11 mg.m⁻³

Example 2

4   The operator works for 8 hours on a process in which he is exposed to a substance hazardous to health. The average exposure during that period is measured as 0.15 mg.m⁻³.

The 8-hour TWA =

$$\frac{(0.15 \times 8)}{8}$$

= 0.15 mg.m⁻³

Example 3

5   Working periods may be split into several sessions for the purpose of sampling to take account of rest and meal breaks etc. This is illustrated by the following example:

Working period	Exposure (mg.m⁻³)	Duration of sampling (h)
0800–1030	0.32	2.5
1045–1245	0.07	2
1330–1530	0.2	2
1545–1715	0.1	1.5

Exposure is assumed to be zero during the periods 1030 to 1045, 1245 to 1330 and 1530 to 1545.

The 8-hour TWA =

$$\frac{(0.32 \times 2.5) + (0.07 \times 2) + (0.20 \times 2) + (0.10 \times 1.5) + (0 \times 1.25)}{8}$$

$$= \frac{0.80 + 0.14 + 0.40 + 0.15 + 0}{8}$$

$$= 0.19 \ mg.m^{-3}$$

Example 4

6   An operator works for 8 hours during the night shift on a process in which he is intermittently exposed to a substance hazardous to health. The operator's work pattern during the working period should be known and the best available data relating to each period of exposure should be applied in calculating the 8-hour TWA. These should be based on direct measurement, estimates based on data already available or reasonable assumptions.

Working period	Task	Exposure (mg.m⁻³)
2200 to 2400	Helping in workshop	0.1 (known to be exposure of full-time group in workshop)
2400 to 0100	Cleaning elsewhere in factory	0 (assumed)
0100 to 0400	Working in canteen	0 (assumed)
0400 to 0600	Cleaning-up after breakdown in workshop	0.21 measured

The 8-hour TWA =

$$\frac{(0.10 \times 2) + (0.21 \times 2) + (0 \times 4)}{8}$$

$$= 0.078 \ mg.m^{-3}$$

Example 5

7   The operator works a 12-hour shift each day for 5 days, and then has seven days' rest. The exposure limits are based on an 8-hour reference period in each 24 hours in which an exposure occurs; the seven days' rest makes no difference. While at work, the operator is exposed to 4 mg.m⁻³.

The 8-hour TWA =

$$\frac{(4 \times 12)}{8}$$

$$= 6 \ mg.m^{-3}$$

The short-term reference period

8   Exposure should be recorded as the average over the specified short-term reference period, normally 15 minutes, and should be determined by sampling over that period. For short emissions of less than the reference period, which still may have the potential to cause harm, appropriate action should be taken to ensure that a 'suitable and sufficient' risk assessment is carried out to ensure that there is no risk to health from such exposures.

Methods of measurement and calculation for determining the fibre concentrations of MMMF

76   These paragraphs reproduce the Notice of Approval which is based on the methods detailed in MDHS59/2 *Machine-made fibres*.[10] **The methods are legally binding because they have been approved by the Health and Safety Commission.**

Notice of approval

The Health and Safety Commission has on 9 November 2004 approved the methods of measurement and calculation set out in the Schedule to this notice for the purpose of determining the fibre concentration of MMMF (also known as man-made mineral fibres, machine-made mineral fibres and man-made vitreous fibres) in air for comparison with the workplace exposure limit specified in the Health and Safety Commission's approved list of workplace exposure limits.

Signed:

SUSAN MAWER
Secretary to the Health and Safety Commission
9 November 2004

The Health and Safety Commission (HSC) and the Health and Safety Executive (HSE) merged on 1 April 2008 to form a single national regulatory body. From that date, the Health and Safety Executive became responsible for approving Codes of Practice, with the consent of the Secretary of State.

Schedule

1   The method shall measure the exposure of employees by sampling in the breathing zone of the employee exposed.

2   'Fibre' means a particle with a length >5 µm, average diameter <3 µm, and a ratio of length to diameter >3 to 1, which can be seen using the system specified in paragraph 3.

3   Fibres shall be counted with a phase contrast microscope of such a quality and maintained in such condition at all times during the use that Block 5 on the HSE/NPL Test Slide Mark II would be visible when used in accordance with the manufacturer's instructions. The microscope shall be tested with the slide frequently enough to establish this. The microscope magnification shall be between 400x and 600x. During counting, the difference in refractive index between the fibres and the medium in which they are immersed shall be between 0.05 and 0.30. The microscopist shall be properly trained in relevant techniques.

4   The results shall be regularly tested by quality assurance procedures to ensure that the results are in satisfactory agreement with the average of results obtained by British laboratories participating in a national quality assurance scheme using the methods specified in paragraphs 1–3.

MONITORING EXPOSURE

77   Regulation 10 of COSHH imposes a duty to monitor the exposure of employees to substances hazardous to health in certain specified situations. Further advice on these requirements may be found in the guidance on monitoring of exposure in the COSHH ACOP. [2]

Personal/workplace air monitoring

78   Sampling strategies may involve measurement of the hazardous substance in the breathing zone of the worker (personal sampling) or in the workplace air. Details of routine sampling strategies for individual substances are outside the scope of this document. However, advice is available in *Monitoring strategies for toxic substances*[11] which provides practical guidance on monitoring substances hazardous to health in air.

79   Methods for the sampling and analysis of many substances which have been assigned WELs are described in the HSE series 'Methods for the Determination of Hazardous Substances' (MDHS). The series also incorporates publications of a more general nature such as method validation protocols and guidance on analytical quality assessment and control.

Biological monitoring (see also Table 2)

80   Biological monitoring can be a very useful complementary technique to air monitoring when air sampling techniques alone may not give a reliable indication of exposure. Biological monitoring is the measurement and assessment of hazardous substances or their metabolites in tissues, secretions, excreta or expired air, or any combination of these, in exposed workers. Measurements reflect absorption of a substance by all routes. Biological monitoring may be particularly useful in circumstances where there is likely to be significant skin absorption and/or gastrointestinal tract uptake following ingestion; where control of exposure depends on respiratory protective equipment; where there is a reasonably well-defined relationship between biological monitoring and effect; or where it gives information on accumulated dose and target organ body burden which is related to toxicity.

81   Biological monitoring guidance values (BMGVs) are set where they are likely to be of practical value, suitable monitoring methods exist and there is sufficient data available. The types of data that are available will vary between substances and therefore the route taken to derive the BMGV will vary between substances. BMGVs are either based on a relationship between biological concentrations and health effects, between biological concentrations and exposure at the level of the WEL, or on data collected from a representative sample of workplaces correctly applying the principles of good occupational hygiene practice.

82   BMGVs are non-statutory and any biological monitoring undertaken in association with a guidance value needs to be conducted on a voluntary basis (ie with the fully informed consent of all concerned). BMGVs are intended to be used as tools in meeting the employer's primary duty to ensure adequate control under COSHH. Where a BMGV is exceeded, it does not necessarily mean that any corresponding airborne standard has been exceeded or that ill health will occur. It is intended that where they are exceeded, this will give an indication that investigation into current control measures and work practices is necessary.

83   Where biological monitoring results are below a particular guidance value, it does not mean that an employer need not take any further action to reduce exposure; BMGVs are not an alternative or replacement for airborne occupational exposure limits. Further guidance can be found in *Biological monitoring in the workplace*.[12]

MIXED EXPOSURES

WELs for mixtures

84   The majority of WELs listed in EH40 are for single compounds or for substances containing a common element or radical, for example, 'tungsten and compounds', and 'isocyanates'. A few of the WELs relate to substances commonly encountered as complex mixtures or compounds, for example 'rubber fume'. The WELs for complex mixtures such as rubber fume and hydrocarbon solvents (see paragraph 85) are without prejudice to any WELs for individual components. If the Safety Data Sheet lists a substance with a WEL, the employer should ensure that the WEL is not exceeded. If the substance is one to which a 'Carc' or 'Sen' notation has been applied or which is assigned one of the hazard statements H334, H340, H350 or H350i, or is listed in Schedule 1 of the COSHH Regulations, or in section C of *Asthmagen? Critical assessments of the evidence for agents implicated in occupational asthma,*[5] or is a substance which the risk assessment has shown to be a potential cause of occupational asthma, there is a requirement to reduce exposure to as low as is reasonably practicable. This requirement applies regardless of whether or not the substance has a WEL.

Hydrocarbon solvents

85   Hydrocarbon solvents are normally supplied as complex mixtures. To assist producers and suppliers of mixed hydrocarbon blends to determine suitable 'in house' occupational exposure limits (OELs), HSE's Advisory Committee on Toxic Substances (ACTS) recommends the procedure detailed in paragraphs 86–89. The supplier may pass this information on to a customer, and should in that case refer to this guidance. The procedure covers aliphatics in the range C_5 to C_{15}, cycloalkanes in the range C_5 to C_{16} and aromatics. This definition does not include halogenated or oxygenated hydrocarbons. The procedure only applies to vapours; mists are excluded.

Reciprocal calculation procedure for mixtures of hydrocarbon solvents

86   'In-house' OELs are derived using the reciprocal calculation procedure (RCP). Thus, the OEL for a mixture is calculated as follows:

$$\frac{1}{OEL_{sol}} = \frac{FR_a}{OEL_a} + \frac{FR_b}{OEL_b} + \frac{FR_n}{OEL_n}$$

where:

OEL_{sol} = occupational exposure limit of the hydrocarbon solvent mixture (in mg.m^{-3})
OEL_a = occupational exposure limit or guidance value of the component 'a' (in mg.m^{-3})
FR_a = fraction (w/w) of component 'a' in the solvent mixture

The OEL$_{sol}$ obtained should be rounded to the nearest number as follows:

OEL$_{sol}$ <100 mg.m^{-3} nearest 25
              100–600 mg.m^{-3} nearest 50
              >600 mg.m^{-3} nearest 200

87   The RCP requires an OEL for each component in a mixture of hydrocarbons. Since for many individual hydrocarbons the data on which an OEL could be based is limited, ACTS agreed to:

(a)   divide hydrocarbons into discrete groups based on structural similarity and critical health effects;

(b)   exclude from these groups hydrocarbons with specific toxicity concerns (eg n-hexane). For these hydrocarbons, WELs are listed in Table 1. These WELs should be used in the RCP;

(c)   assign guidance values to these groups which can then be used in the RCP. It should be noted that guidance values have no legal status and there is no obligation on industry to comply with these values if they possess data indicating another limit is more appropriate.

88   The following values (8-hour TWAs) have been approved by ACTS:

Normal and branched chain alkanes

$C_5 – C_6$ 1800 mg.m^{-3}

$\geq C_7$ 1200 mg.m^{-3}

This group **excludes** n-hexane and n-heptane.

Cycloalkanes

$C_5 – C_6 =$ 1800 mg.m^{-3}

$\geq C_7 =$ 800 mg.m^{-3}

This group **excludes** cyclohexane.

Aromatics
500 mg.m^{-3}

This group **excludes** benzene, toluene, xylene, (o-, m-, p- or mixed isomers), ethylbenzene, trimethylbenzene (all isomers) and cumene.

Example

89   The following is an example of how the RCP is applied. White spirit typically contains the following percentage of hydrocarbons:

52%   alkanes $\geq C_7$
             guidance value = 1200 mg.m^{-3}

27%   cycloalkanes $\geq C_7$
             guidance value = 800 mg.m^{-3}

10%   aromatics
             guidance value = 500 mg.m^{-3}

1% C_8 aromatics (o-, m-, p- xylene
            or mixed isomers) WEL = 220 mg.m^{-3}

10%   trimethylbenzenes WEL = 125 mg.m^{-3}

Using the three guidance values and the WEL values for xylene and trimethylbenzenes, an OEL for white spirit can be obtained as shown:

$$\frac{1}{OEL_{sol}} = \frac{52/100}{1200} + \frac{27/100}{800} + \frac{10/10}{500}$$

$$\frac{1/100}{220} + \frac{10/100}{125}$$

$$\frac{1}{OEL_{sol}} = 1.816 \times 10^{-3}$$

$$OEL_{sol} = 551 \text{ mg.m}^{-3}$$

rounded to the nearest 50 gives an OEL for this particular brand of white spirit of 550 mg m^{-3}.

Effects of mixed exposures

90   In the workplace, workers are frequently subject to a variety of mixed exposures involving solid or liquid aerosols or gases. These can arise as a result of work with materials containing a mixture of substances, or from work with several individual substances, simultaneously or successively, in a work shift. Mixed exposures require careful assessment of their health effects and the appropriateness of control standards. The following paragraphs provide a brief summary of the advice on the application of WELs in these circumstances. In all cases of doubt, specialist advice should be sought.

91   The ways in which the constituent substances of a mixed exposure interact vary considerably. Some mixed exposures involve substances that act on different body tissues or organs, or by different toxicological mechanisms, these various effects being independent of each other. Other mixtures will include substances that act on the same organs, or by similar mechanisms, so that the effects reinforce each other and the substances are additive in their effect. In some cases, the overall effect is considerably greater than the sum of the individual effects, and is synergistic. This may arise from mutual enhancements of the effects of the constituents or because one substance potentiates another, causing it to act in a way which it would not do alone.

Risk assessment and control

92   With all types of mixed exposures it is essential that assessments should be based on the concentrations of each of the constituents in air to which workers are exposed. Depending on the nature of the constituents and the circumstances of use, the relative concentrations of the constituents in air may differ considerably from those in the liquid or solid source material. The composition of the bulk material should not be relied on for assessment unless there is good evidence for doing so.

93   Where mixed exposures occur, the first step is to ensure adequate control of exposure for each individual substance, as outlined in Schedule 2a of the COSHH Regulations.[1] WELs for defined mixtures should be used only where they are applicable and in addition to any relevant individual WELs. They should not be extended to inappropriate situations. It is then necessary to assess whether further control is needed to counteract any increased risk from the substances acting in conjunction. Expert assessments for some particular mixed exposures may be available and can be used as guidelines in similar cases. In other cases, close examination of the toxicological data will be necessary to determine which of the main types of interaction (if any) are likely for the particular combination of substances concerned; the various types should be considered in the following order:

(a)   **Synergistic substances:** Known cases of synergism and potentiation are considerably less common than the other types of behaviour in mixed exposures. However, they are the most serious in their effects and require the most strict control. They are also the most difficult to assess and wherever there is reason to suspect such intervention, specialist advice should be obtained.

(b)   **Additive substances:** Where there is reason to believe that the effects of the constituents are additive, and where the WELs are based on the same health effects, the mixed exposure should be assessed by means of the formula:

$$C_1/L_1 + C_2/L_2 + C_3/L_3 \ldots < 1$$

where C_1, C_2 etc are the time-weighted average (TWA) concentrations of constituents in air and L_1, L_2 are the corresponding WELs. Where the sum of the C/L fractions does not exceed 1, the exposure is considered not to exceed the notional exposure limit. The use of this formula is only applicable where L_1, L_2 etc relate to the same reference period in the list of approved WELs. This formula is not applicable where the lead health effect is cancer or asthma, ie substances to which a 'Carc' or 'Sen' notation has been applied; or to which one of the hazard statements H334, H340, H350 or H350i has been assigned; or to substances listed in Schedule 1 of COSHH; or substances that are listed in section C of *Asthmagen? Critical assessments of the evidence for agents implicated in occupational asthma,*[5] or substances for which the risk assessment has shown to be a potential cause of occupational asthma. For mixtures containing these substances, the overriding duty is to reduce exposure as far as is reasonably practicable (see paragraph 83).

(c)   **Independent substances:** Where no synergistic or additive effects are known or considered likely, the constituents can be regarded as acting independently and the measures needed to achieve adequate control assessed for each separately. The controls needed for the mixture will be those for the component requiring the tightest control.

94   The above steps provide a basic protocol for assessment of mixed exposures. It is open to people responsible for control of exposure to treat all non-synergistic systems as though they were additive. This avoids the need to distinguish additive and independent systems and can be regarded as the more prudent course, particularly where the toxicity data are scarce or difficult to assess.

Monitoring mixed exposure

95   Information on monitoring airborne contaminants is given in *Monitoring strategies for toxic substances.*[11] The number of components of a mixed exposure for which routine air monitoring is required can be reduced if their relative concentrations can be shown to be constant. This involves the selection of a key or marker, which may be one of the constituents, as a measure of the total contamination. Exposure to the marker is controlled at a level selected so that exposures to all components will be controlled in accordance with the criteria in paragraph 93 (a&b). However, if one of the components has been assigned a 'Carc' or 'Sen' notation, or one of the hazard statements H334, H340, H350 or H350i, or is listed in Schedule 1 of the COSHH regulations, or is

listed in section C of *Asthmagen? Critical assessments of the evidence for agents implicated in occupational asthma*,[5] or is a substance for which the risk assessment has shown to be a potential cause of occupational asthma, then the level of the exposure to that substance should always be reduced as far as is reasonably practicable. Monitoring should be under the guidance of suitable specialist advice.

Complicating factors

96   Several factors that complicate the assessment and control of exposure to individual substances will also affect cases of mixed exposures and will require similar special consideration. Such factors include:

(a)   exposure to a substance for which there is no WEL (see paragraphs 147–148 of the COSHH ACOP);[2]

(b)   the relevance of such factors as alcohol, medication, smoking and additional stresses;

(c)   exposure of the skin to one or more substances that can be absorbed by this route as well as by inhalation (see paragraphs 149–151 of the COSHH ACOP);[2] and

(d)   substances in mixtures may mutually affect the extent of their absorption, as well as their health effects, at a given level of exposure.

In each of these circumstances specialist advice should be obtained.

TABLE 2: BIOLOGICAL MONITORING GUIDANCE VALUES (BMGVS)

97   The framework for the use of biological monitoring and the setting of biological monitoring guidance values (BMGVs) is detailed in paragraphs 80–83. For each substance with a BMGV, a free information sheet briefly describing a suggested analytical method, appropriate sampling strategy, the availability of quality assurance schemes and interpretation of results is available. Information sheets can be obtained from the Health and Safety Laboratory www.hsl.gov.uk.

Substance	Biological monitoring guidance values	Sampling time
Butan-2-one	70 µmol butan-2-one/L in urine	Post shift
2-Butoxyethanol	240 mmol butoxyacetic acid/mol creatinine in urine	Post shift
Carbon monoxide	30 ppm carbon monoxide in end-tidal breath	Post shift
Chromium VI	10 µmol chromium/mol creatinine in urine	Post shift
Chlorobenzene	5 mmol 4-chlorocatechol/mol creatinine in urine	Post shift
Cyclohexanone	2 mmol cyclohexanol/mol creatinine in urine	Post shift
Dichloromethane	30 ppm carbon monoxide in end-tidal breath	Post shift
N,N-Dimethylacetamide	100 mmol N-methylacetamide/mol creatinine in urine	Post shift
Glycerol trinitrate (Nitroglycerin)	15 µmol total nitroglycols/mol creatinine in urine	At the end of the period of exposure
Isocyanates (applies to HDI, IPDI, TDI and MDI)	1 µmol isocyanate-derived diamine/mol creatinine in urine	At the end of the period of exposure
Lindane (gBHC(ISO))	35 nmol/L (10 µg/L) of lindane in whole blood (equivalent to 70 nmol/L of lindane in plasma)	Random
MbOCA (2,2' dichloro-4,4' methylene dianiline)	15 µmol total MbOCA/mol creatinine in urine	Post shift
Mercury	20 µmol mercury/mol creatinine in urine	Random
4-methylpentan-2-one	20 µmol 4-methylpentan-2-one/L in urine	Post shift
4,4'-Methylenedianiline (MDA)	50 µmol total MDA/mol creatinine in urine	Post shift for inhalation and pre-shift next day for dermal exposure
Polycyclic aromatic hydrocarbons (PAHs)	4 µmol 1-hydroxypyrene/mol creatinine in urine	Post shift
Xylene, o-, m-, p- or mixed isomers	650 mmol methyl hippuric acid/mol creatinine in urine	Post shift

LIST OF SYNONYMS

Substance	Name it is listed by in Table 1
α-chloropropylene oxide	1-Chloro-2,3-epoxypropane (Epichlorohydrin)
(Diethylamine)ethane	Triethylamine
(S)-3-(1-Methyl-2-pyrrolidinyl)pyridine	Nicotine
1-(1-methylethyl)amino-3-(1-naphthalenoxy) propan-2-ol	Propranolol
1,1,1-trifluoro-2,2-chlorobromoethane	Halothane
1,1'-Azobiscarbamide	Azodicarbonamide
1,1'-Azobisformamide	Azodicarbonamide
1,1-Dichloroethylene	Vinylidene chloride
1,1'-Dimethyl-4,4'-Bipyridinium dichloride	Paraquat dichloride (ISO)
1,1-oxybisethane	Diethyl ether
1,2,3,4,7,7-Hexachloro-1,5,5a,6,9,9a-hexahydro-6,9-methano-2,4,3-benzodioxathiepin-3-oxide	Endosulfan (ISO)
1,2,3-Trimethylbenzene	1,2,3-Trimethylbenzene
1,2,4-Benzenetricarboxylic anhydride	Trimellitic anhydride
1,2,4-TCB	1,2,4-Trichlorobenzene
1,2,4-Trimethylbenzene	1,2,4-Trimethylbenzene
1,2-Benzenedicarboxylic acid dinonyl ester	Dinonyl phthalate
1,2-Benzenedicarboxylic acid, di-2-propenyl ester	Diallyl phthalate
1,2-Benzenedicarboxylic anhydride	Phthalic anhydride
1,2-Benzenediol	Pyrocatechol
1,2-Bis(ethoxycarbonyl)ethyl O,O-dimethyl phosphorodithioate	Malathion (ISO)
1,2-Dichloroethene	1,2-Dichloroethylene, cis:trans isomers 60:40
1,2-Dichlorotetrafluoroethane	Cryofluorane (INN)
1,2-Dihydroxybenzene	Pyrocatechol
1,2-Dihydroxyethane	Ethane-1,2-diol
1,2-Dihydroxypropane	Propane-1,2-diol
1,2-Epoxypropane	Propylene oxide
1,2-Ethanediol	Ethane-1,2-diol
1,3,5-Triglycidyl isocyanurate	Triglycidyl isocyanurate (TGIC)
1,4,7-Tri-(aza)-heptane	2,2'-Iminodi(ethylamine)
1,4-Benzenediamine	p-Phenylenediamine
1,4-Diaminobenzene	p-Phenylenediamine
1,4-Diazacyclohexane	Piperazine
1,4-dichlorobenzene	1,4-dichlorobenzene (para-dichlorobenzene)
1,4-Dihydroxybenzene	Hydroquinone
1,4-Epoxybutane	Tetrahydrofuran
1,7,7-Trimethylnorcamphor	Bornan-2-one
1-Acteoxyethylene	Vinyl acetate
1-Amino-2-methylbenzene	o-Toluidine
1-Aminoethane	Ethylamine
1-Chloro-2,2,2-trifluoroethyldifluoromethyl ether	Isoflurane

Substance	Name it is listed by in Table 1
1-Isopropylamino-3-(1-naphthyloxy)propan-2-ol	Propranolol
1-Methoxy-2-propanol acetate	1-Methoxypropyl acetate
1-Methoxypropylacetate-2-acetic acid	1-Methoxypropyl acetate
1-Methyl-2-aminobenzene	o-Toluidine
1-methyl-2-pyrrolidinone	1-Methyl-2-pyrrolidone
1-Methylethylbenzene	Cumene
1-pentyl acetate	Pentyl acetates (all isomers)
1-Propyl acetate	n-Propyl acetate
2,2-Bis(hydroxymethyl)-1,3-Propanediol	Pentaerythritol
2,4,6-Trinitrophenol	Picric acid
2,4-DES	Sodium 2-(2,4-dichlorophenoxy) ethyl sulphate
2,4-Dichlorophenoxyacetic acid	2,4-D (ISO)
2,5-Furandione	Maleic anhydride
2-Acetoxybenzoic acid	o-Acetylsalicylic acid
2-Acetoxypropane	Isopropyl acetate
2-Aminopyridine	2-Pyridylamine
2-Aminotoluene	o-Toluidine
2-Bromo-2-chloro-1,1,1-trifluroethane	Halothane
2-Butanone	Butan-2-one (methyl ethyl ketone)
2-Chloro-1,1,2-trifluoroethyldifluoromethyl ether	Enflurane
2-Chloro-1-ethanal	Chloroacetaldehyde
2-Ethylhexyl chlorocarbonate	2-Ethylhexyl chloroformate
2-ethylhexan-1-ol	2-ethylhexan-1-ol
2-Furancarboxaldehyde	2-Furaldehyde (furfural)
2-Furanaldehyde	2-Furaldehyde (furfural)
2-Furancarbonal	2-Furaldehyde (furfural)
2-Hexanone	Hexan-2-one
2-Hydroxypropyl acrylate	2-Hydroxypropyl acrylate
2-Isopropoxyphenyl methylcarbamate	Propoxur (ISO)
2-Methoxy-1-methylethylacetate	1-Methoxypropyl acetate
2-Methoxy-2-methylpropane	Methyl-tert-butyl ether
2-Methyl-1-propyl acetate	Isobutyl acetate
2-Methyl-2-propenenitrile	Methacrylonitrile
2-Methyl-2-propenoic acid	Methyl methacrylate
2-Methylaniline	o-Toluidine
2-NP	2-Nitropropane
2-Oxohexamethylenimine	1,6-Hexanolactam (e-caprolactam)
2-Pentyl acetate	Pentyl acetates (all isomers)
2-Phenylpropane	Cumene
2-Propanol	Propan-2-ol
2-Propen-1-ol	Allyl alcohol
2-Propenamide	Acrylamide
2-Propenenitrile	Acrylonitrile
2-Propenoic acid methyl ester	Methyl acrylate
2-Propenoic acid 2-cyano ethyl ester	Ethyl cyanoacrylate
2-Propenoic acid 2-cyano methyl ester	Methyl cyanoacrylate
2-Propenoic acid, n-butyl ester	n-Butyl acrylate
2-Propenoic ethyl ester	Ethyl acrylate

Substance	Name it is listed by in Table 1
2-Toluidine	o-Toluidine
3-(3,4-Dichlorophenyl)-1,1-dimethylurea	Diuron (ISO)
3,3'-Dichloro-4,4'-diaminodiphenyl methane	2,2'-Dichloro-4,4'-methylene dianiline (MbOCA)
3a,4,7,7a-Tetrahydro-4,7-methanoindene	Dicyclopentadiene
3-Heptanone	Heptan-3-one
3-Hydroxypropene	Allyl alcohol
3-pentyl acetate	Pentyl acetates (all isomers)
4,4'-Diaminodiphenylmethane	4,4'-Methylenedianiline
4,4'-Diamino-3,3'-dichlorodiphenylmethane	2,2'-Dichloro-4,4'-methylene dianiline (MbOCA)
4,4'-Isopropylidenediphenol	Bisphenol A
4,4-Methylene bis(2-chloroaniline)	2,2'-Dichloro-4,4'-methylene dianiline (MbOCA)
4,4'-(propane-2,2-diyl)diphenol	Bisphenol A
4,4'-Thiobis(6-tert-butyl-m-cresol)	6,6'-Di-*tert*-butyl-4,4'-thiodi-*m*-cresol
4-Acetamidophenol	Paracetamol
4-Amino-3,5,6-trichloropyridine-2-carboxylic acid	Picloram (ISO)
4-Hydroxyacetanilide	Paracetamol
5-Bromo-3-sec-butyl-6-methyluracil	Bromacil (ISO)
Acetaminophen	Paracetamol
Acetanhydride	Acetic anhydr
Acetic acid	Acetic acid
Acetic acid amyl ester	Pentyl acetates (all isomers)
Acctic acid anhydride	Acetic anhydride
Acetic acid dimethylamide	*NN*-Dimethylacetamide
Acetic acid, 1,1-dimethylethyl ester	*tert*-Butyl acetate
Acetic acid, ethenyl ester	Vinyl acetate
Acetic acid vinyl ester	Vinyl acetate
Acetic aldehyde	Acetaldehyde
Acetic oxide	Acetic anhydride
Acetyl ether	Acetic anhydride
Acetyl oxide	Acetic anhydride
Acetylene dichloride	1,2-Dichloroethylene, cis:trans isomers 60:40
Acetylene tetrabromide	1,1,2,2-Tetrabromoethane
Acrolein	Acrylaldehyde (Acrolein)
Acrylaldehyde (Acrolein)	Acrylaldehyde (Acrolein)
Acrylic acid	Acrylic acid
Acrylic acid 2-cyano ethyl ester	Ethyl cyanoacrylate
Acrylic acid 2-cyano methyl ester	Methyl cyanoacrylate
Acrylic acid, n-butyl ester	*n*-Butyl acrylate
ACT	Benzyl chloride
alpha-Chlorotoluene	Benzyl chloride
alpha-Methyl styrene	2-Phenylpropene
Alumina	Aluminium oxides
Aluminium alkyl compounds	Aluminium alkyl compounds
Aluminium metal	Aluminium metal
Aluminium salts, soluble	Aluminium salts, soluble
Alumite	Aluminium oxides
Aminobenzene	Aniline
Aminocaprolactam	1,6-Hexanolactam (e-caprolactam)

Substance	Name it is listed by in Table 1
Aminocyclohexane	Cyclohexylamine
Aminoethane	Ethylamine
Amitrole	Amitrole
Ammonia, anhydrous	Ammonia, anhydrous
Ammonium chloride, fume	Ammonium chloride, fume
Ammonium hexachloroplantinate	Halogeno-platinum compounds (as Pt)
Ammonium sulphamate	Ammonium sulphamidate
Ammonium tetrachloroplantinate	Halogeno-platinum compounds (as Pt)
Amyl acetates (all isomers)	Pentyl acetates (all isomers)
Amyl ethyl ketone	5-Methylheptan-3-one
Amylmethylketone	Heptan-2-one
Antimony and compounds except stibine (as Sb)	Antimony and compounds except stibine (as Sb)
Araldite PT-810	Triglycidyl isocyanurate (TGIC)
Arcton 22	Chlorodifluoromethane
Aroclor	Polychlorinated biphenyls (PCB)
Arsenic and arsenic compounds except arsine (as As)	Arsenic and arsenic compounds except arsine (as As)
Arsenic trihydride	Arsine
Arylamine	Aniline
Asphalt, petroleum fumes	Asphalt, petroleum fumes
Aspirin	o-Acetylsalicylic acid
Azabenzene	Pyridine
Azacyclohexane	Piperidine
Barite	Barium sulphate
Barium compounds	Barium compounds
Barytes	Barium sulphate
BCME	Bis(chloromethyl ether)
Benzenamine	Aniline
Benzene chloride	Chlorobenzene
Benzol	Benzene
Benzoyl peroxide	Dibenzoyl peroxide
Beryllium and beryllium compounds (as Be)	Beryllium and beryllium compounds (as Be)
Beta-propanolol	Propranolol
Bicyclo(2,2,1)heptan-2-one	Bornan-2-one
Bismuth telluride	Dibismuth tritelluride
Bisphenol A	Bisphenol A
Bladafum	Sulfotep (ISO)
Blanc fixe	Barium sulphate
Borates, (tetra) sodium salts	Disodium tetraborate, anhydrous
Borates, (tetra) sodium salts	Disodium tetraborate, decahydrate
Borates, (tetra) sodium salts	Disodium tetraborate, pentahydrate
Boron oxide	Diboron trioxide
Boron tribromide	Boron tribromide
Bromine	Bromine
But-2-yne-1,4-diol	But-2-yne-1,4-diol
Butane	Butane
Butanedione	Diacetyl
Butanone	Butan-2-one (methyl ethyl ketone)
Butyl acrylate	n-Butyl acrylate

Substance	Name it is listed by in Table 1
Butyl benzyl phthalate	Benzyl butyl phthalate
Butyl cellosolve	2-Butoxyethanol
Butyl cellosolve acetate	2-Butoxyethyl acetate
Butyl ethyl ketone	Heptan-3-one
Butyl glycol	2-Butoxyethanol
Butyl glycol acetate	2-Butoxyethyl acetate
Butyl methyl ketone	Hexan-2-one
Butyl oxitol	2-Butoxyethanol
Butyl phosphate	Tributyl phosphate, all isomers
Butylated hydroxytoluene	2,6-Di-*tert*-butyl-*p*-cresol
Butylene oxide	Tetrahydrofuran
Butylglycol acetate	2-Butoxyethyl acetate
C,C'-azodi(formamide)	Azodicarbonamide
Cadmium and cadmium compounds except cadmium oxide fume, cadmium sulphide and cadmium sulphide pigments (as Cd)	Cadmium and cadmium compounds except cadmium oxide fume, cadmium sulphide and cadmium sulphide pigments (as Cd)
Cadmium oxide fume (as Cd)	Cadmium oxide fume (as Cd)
Cadmium sulphide and cadmium sulphide pigments (respirable dust (as Cd))	Cadmium sulphide and cadmium sulphide pigments (respirable dust (as Cd))
Caesium hydroxide	Caesium hydroxide
Calcite	Marble
Calcium carbonate	Calcium carbonate
Calcium cyanamide	Calcium cyanamide
Calcium hydroxide	Calcium hydroxide
Calcium dihydroxide	Calcium hydroxide
Calcium oxide	Calcium oxide
Calcium silicate	Calcium silicate
Calcium sulphate	Gypsum
Calcium sulphate	Plaster of Paris
Camphor, synthetic	Bornan-2-one
Caprolactam	1,6-Hexanolactam (e-caprolactam)
Carbamaldehyde	Formamide
Carbimides	Isocyanates
Carbodiimide	Cyanamide
Carbon bisulphide	Carbon disulphide
Carbon black	Carbon black
Carbon monoxide	Carbon monoxide
Carbon oxychloride	Phosgene
Carbon tetrachloride	Carbon tetrachloride
Carbonic anhydride	Carbon dioxide
Carbonic oxide	Carbon monoxide
Carbonimides	Isocyanates
Carbonyl chloride	Phosgene
Carbylamines	Isocyanates
Catechol	Pyrocatechol
Cellosolve	2-Ethoxyethanol
Cellosolve acetate	2-Ethoxyethyl acetate
Cellulose	Cellulose (pure)
Cement dust	Portland cement
CFC-114	Cryofluorane (INN)
Chlorinated biphenyls	Polychlorinated biphenyls (PCB)

Substance	Name it is listed by in Table 1
Chlorine	Chlorine
Chlorine (IV) oxide	Chlorine dioxide
Chlorine oxide	Chlorine dioxide
Chlorine peroxide	Chlorine dioxide
Chloroacetic acid	Monochloroacetic acid
Chlorobenzol	Chlorobenzene
Chlorocyanogen	Cyanogen chloride
Chloroethylene	Vinyl chloride
Chloromethyl ether	Bis (chloromethyl ether)
Chloromethyloxirane	1-Chloro-2,3-epoxypropane (Epichlorohydrin)
Chlorophenylmethane	Benzyl chloride
Chlorosulphonic acid	Chlorosulphonic acid
Chromium	Chromium
Chromium (II) compounds	Chromium (II) compounds
Chromium (III) compounds	Chromium (III) compounds
Chromium (VI) compounds (as Cr)	Chromium (VI) compounds (as Cr)
Cinerin	Pyrethrins (ISO)
cis-Butenedioic anhydride	Maleic anhydride
Cobalt and cobalt compounds (as Co)	Cobalt and cobalt compounds (as Co)
Colophony	Rosin-based solder flux fume
Copper	Copper
Cotton dust	Cotton dust
Cristobalite, respirable dust	Silica, respirable crystalline
Crystalline silica, respirable dust	Silica, respirable crystalline
Cyanides, except HCN, cyanogen and cyanogen chloride	Cyanides, except HCN, cyanogen and cyanogen chloride
Cyanoethylene	Acrylonitrile
Cyanolit	Methyl cyanoacrylate
Cyanomethane	Acetonitrile
Cyclohexane	Cyclohexane
Cyclohexanone isooxime	1,6-Hexanolactam (e-caprolactam)
Dactin	1,3-Dichloro-5,5-dimethyl-hydantoin
DADPM	4,4'-Methylenedianiline
DDM	4,4'-Methylenedianiline
DEHP	Bis(2-ethylhexyl) phthalate
Derris, commercial	Rotenone (ISO)
Diacetone alcohol	4-Hydroxy-4-methylpentan-2-one
Diacetyl	Diacetyl
Dialkyl 79 phthalate	Dialkyl 79 phthalate
Diamine	Hydrazine
Diatomaceous earth, natural, respirable dust	Diatomaceous earth, natural, respirable dust
Diazenedicarboxamide	Azodicarbonamide
Dibutyl phthalate	Dibutyl phthalate
Dichloroacetylene	Dichloroacetylene
Dichloromethane	Dichloromethane
Dicyclohexyl phthalate	Dicyclohexyl phthalate
Diethyl ketone	Pentan-3-one
Diethyl oxide	Diethyl ether
Diethyl phthalate	Diethyl phthalate

Substance	Name it is listed by in Table 1
Diethylene glycol	2,2'-Oxydiethanol
Diethylene imidoximine	Morpholine
Diethylene oxide	Tetrahydrofuran
Diethylene oximine	Morpholine
Diethylene triamine	2,2'-Iminodi(ethylamine)
Diethylenediamine	Piperazine
Diethylenediamine dihydrochloride	Piperazine dihydrochloride
Diethyleneimine	Piperazine
Difluorochloromethane	Chlorodifluoromethane
Diisobutyl ketone	2,6-Dimethylheptan-4-one
Diisobutyl phthalate	Diisobutyl phthalate
Diisodecyl phthalate	Diisodecyl phthalate
Diisononyl phthalate	Diisononyl phthalate
Diisooctyl phthalate	Diisooctyl phthalate
Diisopropylamine	Diisopropylamine
Dihydrogen sulphate	Sulphuric acid
Dimethyl ketone	Acetone
Dimethyl phthalate	Dimethyl phthalate
Dimethyl sulphate	Dimethyl sulphate
Dimethylbenzene	Xylene, o-,m-,p- or mixed isomers
Dimethylethanolamine	Dimethylaminoethanol
Dimethylethylamine	N,N-Dimethylethylamine
Dimethylnitromethane	2-Nitropropane
Di-n-butyl phosphate	Dibutyl hydrogen phosphate
Dinitrobenzene, all isomers	Dinitrobenzene, all isomers
Dinitrogen monoxide	Nitrous oxide
Diothionic acid	Sulphuric acid
Dioxan	1,4-Dioxane
Diphenylamine	Diphenylamine
Diphenyl ether	Diphenyl ether
Dipropylene glycol methyl ether	(2-methoxymethylethoxy) propanol
Dipropylene glycol monomethyl ether	(2-methoxymethylethoxy) propanol
Dipropylmethane	n-Heptane
Dipyrido[1,2-a:2',1'-c]pyrazinediium, 6,7-dihydro-,	Diquat dibromide (ISO) dibromide
Di-sec-octyl phthalate	Bis(2-ethylhexyl) phthalate
Dithiocarbonic anhydride	Carbon disulphide
Dithiofos	Sulfotep (ISO)
Dithiophosphoric acid, tetraethyl ester	Sulfotep (ISO)
Dithiotep	Sulfotep (ISO)
Divanadium pentoxide	Vanadium pentoxide
DMA	NN-Dimethylacetamide
DMAc	NN-Dimethylacetamide
DMAE Dimethylaminoethanol DME	Dimethyl ether
DMEA	Dimethylaminoethanol
DMF	Dimethylformamide
DMS	Dimethyl sulphate
DPGME	(2-methoxymethylethoxy) propanol
Dursban	Chlorpyrifos (ISO)

Substance	Name it is listed by in Table 1
EAK	5-Methylheptan-3-one
EBK	Heptan-3-one
ECA	Ethyl cyanoacrylate
e-Caprolactam	1,6-Hexanolactam (e-caprolactam)
ECH	1-Chloro-2,3-epoxypropane (Epichlorohydrin)
EDB	1,2-Dibromoethane (Ethylene dibromide)
Emery	Emery
Enthrane	Enflurane
Epichlorohydrin	1-Chloro-2,3-epoxypropane (Epichlorohydrin)
Epoxyethane	Ethylene oxide
Ethanal	Acetaldehyde
Ethanamine	Ethylamine
Ethanedioic acid	Oxalic acid
Ethanediol	Ethane-1,2-diol
Ethanoic anhydride	Acetic anhydride
Ethanolamine	2-Aminoethanol
Ethenyl acetate	Vinyl acetate
Ether	Diethyl ether
Ether hydrochloric	Chlorethane
Ethrane	Enflurane
Ethyl 2-propenoate	Ethyl acrylate
Ethyl acetate	Ethyl acetate
Ethyl acetate ester	Ethyl acetate
Ethyl alcohol	Ethanol
Ethyl aldehyde	Acetaldehyde
Ethyl amyl ketone	5-Methylheptan-3-one
Ethyl butyl ketone	Heptan-3-one
Ethyl chloride	Chloroethane
Ethyl chlorocarbonate	Ethyl chloroformate
Ethyl ethanoate	Ethyl acetate
Ethyl ether	Diethyl ether
Ethyl mercaptan	Ethanethiol
Ethyl methanoate	Ethyl formate
Ethyl oxide	Diethyl ether
Ethyl thiopyrophosphate	Sulfotep (ISO)
Ethyl-2-cyano-2-propenoate	Ethyl cyanoacrylate
Ethyl-2-cyanoacrylate	Ethyl cyanoacrylate
Ethylene chlorohydrin	2-Chloroethanol
Ethylene dibromide	1,2-Dibromoethane (Ethylene dibromide)
Ethylene dichloride	1,2-Dichloroethane (Ethylene dichloride)
Ethylene glycol	Ethane-1,2-diol
Ethylene glycol dimethyl ether	Dimethoxymethane
Ethylene glycol monobutyl ether	2-Butoxyethanol
Ethylene glycol monobutyl ether acetate	2-Butoxyethyl acetate
Ethylene glycol monoethyl ether	2-Ethoxyethanol
Ethylene glycol monoethyl ether acetate	2-Ethoxyethyl acetate
Ethylene glycol monomethyl ether	2-Methoxyethanol
Ethylene glycol monomethyl ether acetate	2-Methoxyethyl acetate

Substance	Name it is listed by in Table 1
Ethylene tetrachloride	Tetrachloroethylene
Ethylidene chloride	1,1-Dichloroethane
Ethylidene dichloride	1,1-Dichloroethane
Ferric oxide	Rouge
Ferrous foundry particulate	Ferrous foundry particulate
Flour dust	Flour Dust
Flue gas	Carbon monoxide
Fluoride (inorganic as F)	Fluoride (inorganic as F)
Fluorine	Fluorine
Fluothane	Halothane
Forane	Isoflurane
Freon 123B1	Halothane
Freon 134a	1,1,1,2-Tetrafluoroethane (HFC 134a)
Freon 22	Chlorodifluoromethane
Fural	2-furaldehyde (furfural)
Furfural	2-furaldehyde (furfural)
Furfuraldehyde	2-furaldehyde (furfural)
Germanium tetrahydride	Germane
Glutaral	Glutaraldehyde
Glutardialdehyde	Glutaraldehyde
Glutaric dialdehyde	Glutaraldehyde
Glycerin, mist	Glycerol, mist
Glycerol trinitrate	Glycerol trinitrate
Glycol	Ethane-1,2-diol
Grain dust	Grain dust
Graphite	Graphite
Halane	1,3-Dichloro-5,5-dimethyl-hydantoin
Halogeno-platinum compounds (complex co-ordination compounds in which the platinum atom is directly co-ordinated to halide groups) (as Pt)	Halogeno-platinum compounds (complex co-ordination compounds in which the platinum atom is directly co-ordinated to halide groups) (as Pt)
Hardwood dust	Hardwood dust
HCFC 22	Chlorodifluoromethane
HCFC-21	Dichlorofluoromethane
Heavy spar	Barium sulphate
Hexahydro-1,4-diazine	Piperazine
Hexahydro-2H-azepin-2-one	1,6-Hexanolactam (e-caprolactam)
Hexahydrobenzene	Cyclohexane
Hexahydropyrazine	Piperazine
Hexalin	Cyclohexanol
Hexamethylene	Cyclohexane
Hexane	n-Hexane
Hexanon	Cyclohexanone
Hexylene glycol	2-Methylpentane-2,4-diol
HFC 134a	1,1,1,2-Tetrafluoroethane
Hydrobromic acid	Hydrogen bromide
Hydrobromic gas	Hydrogen bromide
Hydrochloric acid	Hydrogen chloride (gas and aerosol mists)
Hydrocyanic acid	Hydrogen cyanide
Hydrofluoric acid	Hydrogen fluoride (as F)
Hydrofuran	Tetrahydrofuran

Substance	Name it is listed by in Table 1
Hydrogen cyanide	Hydrogen cyanide
Hydrogen peroxide	Hydrogen peroxide
Hydrogen phosphide	Phosphine
Hydrogen selenide	Dihydrogen selenide (as Se)
Hydrosulphuric acid	Hydrogen sulphide
Hydrous magnesium silicate	Talc
Hydroxybenzene	Phenol
Indium and compounds (as In)	Indium and compounds (as In)
Indonaphthene	Indene
Iodine	Iodine
Iron oxide, fume (as Fe)	Iron oxide, fume (as Fe)
Iron pentacarbonyl (as Fe)	Pentacarbonyliron (as Fe)
Iron salts (as Fe)	Iron salts (as Fe)
Isoamyl alcohol	3-Methylbutan-1-ol
Isoamyl methyl ketone	5-Methylhexan-2-one
Isobutyl alcohol	2-Methylpropan-1-ol
Isocyanates, all (as –NCO)	Isocyanates, all (as –NCO)
Isocyanic acid esters	Isocyanates
Isonitropropane	2-Nitropropane
Isooctanol	Isooctyl alcohol (mixed isomers)
Isopentyl acetate	Pentyl acetates (all isomers)
Isopentyl methyl ketone	5-Methylhexan-2-one
Isophorone	3,5,5-trimethylcyclohex-2-enone
Isopropanol	Propan-2-ol
Isopropyl acetone	4-Methylpentan-2-one
Isopropyl alcohol	Propan-2-ol
Isopropyl chlorocarbonate	Isopropyl chloroformate
Isopropyl ether	Diisopropyl ether
Isopropylbenzene	Cumene
Jasmolin	Pyrethrins (ISO)
Kaolin, respirable dust	Kaolin, respirable dust
Ketohexamethylene	Cyclohexanone
Laughing gas	Nitrous oxide
Limestone	Limestone
Lithium hydride	Lithium hydride
Lithium hydroxide	Lithium hydroxide
LPG	Liquefied petroleum gas
Magnesia	Magnesium oxide (as Mg)
Magnesium carbonate	Magnesite
Maleic acid anhydride	Maleic anhydride
Manganese and its inorganic compounds	Manganese and its inorganic compounds
MbOCA	2,2'-Dichloro-4,4'-methylene dianiline (MbOCA)
MCA	Methyl cyanoacrylate
MDA	4,4'-Methylenedianiline
m-Dihydroxybenzene	Resorcinol
Mecrylate	Methyl cyanoacrylate
MEK	Butan-2-one (methyl ethyl ketone)
MEKP	Methyl ethyl ketone peroxides (MEKP)

Substance	Name it is listed by in Table 1
Methacide	Toluene
Methacrylic acid methyl ester	Methyl methacrylate
Methanal	Formaldehyde
Methanamide	Formamide
Methane trichloride	Chloroform
Methanoic acid	Formic acid
Methoxycarbonylethylene	Methyl acrylate
Methyl 2-methyl-2-propenoate	Methyl methacrylate
Methyl acetate	Methyl acetate
Methyl alcohol	Methanol
Methyl aldehyde	Formaldehyde
Methyl bromide	Bromomethane
Methyl butyl ketone	Hexan-2-one
Methyl cellosolve	2-Methoxyethanol
Methyl cellosolve acetate	2-Methoxyethyl acetate
Methyl chloride	Chloromethane
Methyl chloroform	1,1,1-Trichloroethane
Methyl ester	Methyl methacrylate
Methyl ether	Dimethyl ether
Methyl ethyl ketone	Butan-2-one (methyl ethyl ketone)
Methyl ethylene oxid	Propylene oxid
Methyl formate	Methyl formate
Methyl iodide	Iodomethane
Methyl isoamyl ketone	5-Methylhexan-2-one
Methyl isobutyl carbinol	4-Methylpentan-2-ol
Methyl isobutyl ketone	4-Methyl-pentan-2-one
Methyl ketone	Acetone
Methyl mercaptan	Methanethiol
Methyl n-butyl ketone	Hexan-2-one
Methyl phosphite	Trimethyl phosphite
Methyl propenoate	Methyl acrylate
Methyl propyl ketone	Pentan-2-one
Methyl-1,1-dimethethyl ether	Methyl-tert-butyl ether
Methyl-2-cyano-propenoate	Methyl cyanoacrylate
Methyl-2-cyanoacrylate	Methyl cyanoacrylate
Methylacetic acid	Propionic acid
Methylacetone	Butan-2-one (methyl ethyl ketone)
Methylal	Dimethoxymethane
Methylamylketone	Heptan-2-one
Methylaniline	N-Methylaniline
Methylbenzene	Toulene
Methylbutyl acetate	Pentyl acetates (all isomers)
Methyldichloromethane	1,1-Dichloroethane
Methylene chloride	Dichloromethane
Methylene oxide	Formaldehyde
Methylene-bis-orthochloroaniline MbOCA	2,2'-Dichloro-4,4'-methylene dianiline MbOCA)
Methylhexalin	Methylcyclohexanol
Methyloxirane	Propylene oxide

Substance	Name it is listed by in Table 1
MIAK	5-Methylhexan-2-one
MIBK	4-Methylpentan-2-one
MMMFs	MMMF (machine-made mineral fibre) (except for refractory ceramic fibres and special purpose fibres)
Molybdenum compounds (as Mo)	Molybdenum compounds (as Mo)
Monochlorobenzene	Chlorobenzene
Monochlorodifluoromethane	Chlorodifluoromethane
Monoethylamine	Ethylamine
M-Pyrol	1-Methyl-2-pyrrolidone
MTBE	Methyl-*tert*-butyl ether
Muriatic acid	Hydrogen chloride (gas and aerosol mists)
N-(4-Hydroxyphenyl)acetamide	Paracetamol
N,N-diethylethanamine	Triethylamine
N,N-Diethylethanolamine	2-Dimethylaminoethanol
N,N-Dimethylethanolamine	2-Dimethylaminoethanol
N,N-Dimethylformamide	*N,N*-Dimethylformamide
Nadone	Cyclohexanone
n-Butanol	Butan-1-ol
n-Butyl acetate	Butyl acetate
n-Butyl alcohol	Butan-1-ol
n-Butyl chlorocarbonate	*n*-Butyl chloroformate
n-Butyl lactate	Butyl lactate
N-Diethylaminoethanol	2-Dimethylaminoethanol
N-Ethylethanamine	Diethylamine
N-Ethylmorpholine	4-Ethylmorpholine
Nickel and its inorganic compounds (except nickel tetracarbonyl): water-soluble nickel compounds (as Ni) nickel and water-insoluble nickel compounds (as Ni)	Nickel and its inorganic compounds (except nickel tetracarbonyl): water-soluble nickel compounds (as Ni) nickel and water-insoluble nickel compounds (as Ni)
Nickel carbonyl	Tetracarbonylnickel (as Ni)
Nitric acid	Nitric acid
Nitrobenzol	Nitrobenzene
Nitroethane	Nitroethane
Nitrogen dioxide	Nitrogen dioxide
Nitrogen monoxide	Nitrogen monoxide
Nitroisopropane	2-Nitropropane
Nitromethane	Nitromethane
N-methyl-2-pyrrolidinone	1-Methyl-2-pyrrolidone
N-Methylmethanamine	Dimethylamine
N-methylpyrrolidone	1-Methyl-2-pyrrolidone
n-Propanol	Propan-1-ol
N-Trichloromethylmercapto-4-cyclohexene-1,2dicarboximide	Captan (ISO)
O,O,O',O'-Tetraethyldithio-pyrophosphate	Sulfotep (ISO)
O,O-Diethyl O-3,5,6-trichloro-2-pyridyl phosphorothioate	Chlorpyrifos (ISO)
O,O-Diethyl S-ethylthiomethyl phosphorodithioate	Phorate (ISO)
o-Dichlorobenzene	1,2-Dichlorobenzene (*ortho*-dichlorobenzene)
omega-Chlorotoluene	Benzyl chloride
o-Methylcyclohexanone	2-Methylcyclohexanone
Orsin	*p*-Phenylenediamine
ortho-Dichlorobenzene	1,2-Dichlorobenzene (*ortho*-dichlorobenzene)
o-sec-Butylphenol	2-*sec*-Butylphenol

Substance	Name it is listed by in Table 1
Osmium tetraoxide (as Os)	Osmium tetraoxide (as Os)
Oxirane	Ethylene oxide
Oxomethane	Formaldehyde
Oxybis(chloromethane)	Bis(chloromethyl ether)
Oxybismethane	Dimethyl ether
Oxymethylene	Formaldehyde
p-Aminoaniline	*p*-Phenylenediamine
para-Dichlorobenzene	1,4-Dichlorobenzene (*para*-dichlorobenzene)
Paraffin wax, fume	Paraffin wax, fume
PCBs	Polychlorinated biphenyls (PCB)
p-Chloronitrobenzene	1-Chloro-4-nitrobenzene
p-Dichlorobenzene	1,4-Dichlorobenzene (*para*-dichlorobenzene)
Pentan-1,5-dial	Glutaraldehyde
Perc	Tetrachloroethylene
Perchloroethylene	Tetrachloroethylene
Periclase	Magnesium oxide (as Mg)
PGME	1-Methoxypropan-2-ol
PGMEA	1-Methoxypropyl acetate
Phenacyl chloride 2-Chloroacetophenone Phenyl chloride	Chlorobenzene
Phenyl ether	Diphenyl ether
Phenylamine	Aniline
Phenylethane	Ethylbenzene
Phenylethylene	Styrene
Phenylmethane	Toluene
Phosphoric acid	Orthophosphoric acid
Phosphoric chloride	Phosphorus pentachloride
Phosphorous chloride	Phosphorus trichloride
Phosphorus (V) oxide	Diphosphorus pentoxide
Phosphorus pentasulphide	Diphosphorus pentasulphide
Phosphorus pentoxide	Diphosphorus pentoxide
Phosphorus perchloride	Phosphorus pentachloride
Phosphorus trihydride	Phosphine
Phosphorus, yellow	Phosphorus, yellow
Phosphoryl trichloride	Phosphoryl trichloride
Phosphorus pentoxide	Diphosphorus pentoxide
Phthalic acid anhydride	Phthalic anhydride
Pimelic ketone	Cyclohexanone
Piperazidine	Piperazine
Piperazine hydrochloride	Piperazine dihydrochloride
Platinum compounds, soluble (except certain halogeno-Pt compounds) (as Pt)	Platinum compounds, soluble (except certain (as Pt) halogeno-Pt compounds)
Platinum metal	Platinum metal
p-Nitrochlorobenzene 1-Chloro-4-nitrobenzene Polychlorobiphenyls	Polychlorinated biphenyls (PCB)
Polymeric aromatic amide derivative	*p*-Aramid respirable fibres
Potassium cyanide	Potassium cyanide
Potassium hydroxide	Potassium hydroxide
p-Phenylene terephthalamide	*p*-Aramid respirable fibres
Precipitator ash	Pulverised fuel ash
Prop-2-enal	Acrylaldehyde (Acrolein)

Substance	Name it is listed by in Table 1
Prop-2-enoic acid	Acrylic acid
Propan-2-one	Acetone
Propanoic acid	Propionic acid
Propanone	Acetone
Propene oxide	Propylene oxide
Propenol	Allyl alcohol
Propenol alcohol	Allyl alcohol
Propionic acid	Propionic acid
Propylene glycol	Propane-1,2-diol
Propylene glycol methyl ether	1-Methoxypropan-2-ol
Propylene glycol methyl ether acetate	1-Methoxypropyl acetate
Propylene glycol-1-monomethyl ether	1-Methoxypropan-2-ol
Propylene glycol-1-monomethylether-2-acetate	1-Methoxypropyl acetate
Prussic acid	Hydrogen cyanide
PVC	Polyvinyl chloride
Pyrazine hexahydride	Piperazine
Pyrethrin	Pyrethrins (ISO)
Pyrethrins (Pyrethrum)	Pyrethrins (Pyrethrum)
Pyridinecarboxylic acid	Picloram (ISO)
Pyromucic aldehyde	2-furaldehyde (furfural)
Quartz, crystyalline	Silica, respirable crystalline
Quinol	Hydroquinone
RCF	Refractory Ceramic Fibres and Special Purpose Fibres
Resorcin	Resorcinol
Respirable Crystalline Silica (RCS)	Respirable Crystalline Silica (RCS)
Rhodium (as Rh)	Rhodium (as Rh)
Rubber fume	Rubber fume
Rubber process dust	Rubber process dust
sec-Butanol	Butan-2-ol
sec-Butyl acetate	sec-Butyl acetate
sec-Butyl alcohol	Butan-2-ol
Selane	Dihydrogen selenide (as Se)
Selenium and compounds, except hydrogen selenide (as Se)	Selenium and compounds, except hydrogen selenide (as Se)
Selenium dihydride	Dihydrogen selenide (as Se)
Selenium hydride	Dihydrogen selenide (as Se)
Sextone	Cyclohexanone
Silane	Silane
Silica, amorphous	Silica, amorphous
Silica, fused respirable dust	Silica, fused respirable dust
Silicon	Silicon
Silicon carbide (not whiskers)	Silicon carbide (not whiskers)
Silver (soluble compounds as Ag)	Silver (soluble compounds as Ag)
Silver compounds	Silver compounds
Silver, metallic	Silver, metallic
Soapstone	Mica
Sodium azide (as NaN_3)	Sodium azide (as NaN_3)
Sodium bisulphite	Sodium hydrogen sulphite
Sodium cyanide	Sodium cyanide

Substance	Name it is listed by in Table 1
Sodium hydroxide	Sodium hydroxide
Sodium metabisulphite	Disodium disulphite
Sodium pyrophosphate	Tetrasodium pyrophosphate
Softwood dust	Softwood dust
Starch	Starch
Styrol	Styrene
Subtilisins	Subtilisins
Sulphur dioxide	Sulphur dioxide
Sulphur hexafluoride	Sulphur hexafluoride
Sulphur monochloride	Disulphur dichloride
Sulphur oxychloride	Thionyl chloride
Sulphuretted hydrogen	Hydrogen sulphide
Sulphuric acid diethyl ester	Diethyl sulphate
Sulphuric acid, dimethyl ester	Dimethyl sulphate
Sulphuric acid (mist)	Sulphuric acid (mist)
Sulphuryl fluoride	Sulphuryl difluoride
Sulphuric oxyfluoride	Sulphuryl difluoride
sym-Dichlorodimethyl ether	Bis (chloromethyl ether)
sym-Dichloroethane	1,2-Dichloroethane (Ethylene dichloride)
sym-Dichoroethylene	2-Dichloroethylene, cist:rans isomers 60:40
Talc, respirable dust	Talc, respirable dust
Talcum	Talc
Tantalum	Tantalum
TEDP	Sulfotep (ISO)
Tellurium and compounds, except hydrogen telluride, (as Te)	Tellurium and compounds, except hydrogen telluride, (as Te)
Terphenyls, all isomers	Terphenyls, all isomers
Terphenyl, hydrogenated	Terphenyl, hydrogenated
tert-amyl acetate	Pentyl acetates (all isomers)
tert-Butyl alcohol	2-Methylpropan-2-ol
tert-Butyl methyl ether	Methyl-tert-butyl ether
Tertiary-butyl-methyl-ether	Methyl-tert-butyl ether
Tetrachloroethene	Tetrachloroethylene
Tetrachloromethane	Carbon tetrachloride
Tetraethyl orthosilicate	Tetraethyl orthosilicate
Tetrahydro-1,4-oxazine	Morpholine
TGIC	Triglycidyl isocyanurate (TGIC)
Thallium, soluble compounds (as Tl)	Thallium, soluble compounds (as Tl)
Thioglycolic acid	Mercaptoacetic acid
Thiosulfan	Endosulfan (ISO)
Tin compounds, inorganic, except SnH$_4$, (as Sn)	Tin compounds, inorganic, except SnH$_4$, (as Sn)
Tin compounds, organic, except Cyhexatin (ISO), (as Sn)	Tin compounds, organic, except Cyhexatin (ISO), (as Sn)
Titanium dioxide	Titanium dioxide
TMA	Trimellitic anhydride
TNT	2,4,6-Trinitrotoluene
Toluol	Toluene
Tolyl chloride	Benzyl chloride
Tosyl chloride	p-Toluenesulphonyl chloride
Toxilic anhydride	Maleic anhydride

Substance	Name it is listed by in Table 1
Triatomic oxygen	Ozone
Trichloroethene	Trichloroethylene
Trichloromethane	Chloroform
Triiodomethane	Iodoform
Trike	Trichloroethylene
Trilene	Trichloroethylene
Trimethylbenzenes, all isomers or mixtures	Trimethylbenzenes, all isomers or mixtures
Tri-*o*-cresyl phosphate	Tri-*o*-tolyl phosphate
Triphenyl phosphate	Triphenyl phosphate
Tripoli, respirable dust	Silica, respirable crystalline
Trydimite, respirable dust	Silica, respirable crystalline
Tungsten and compounds (as W)	Tungsten and compounds (as W)
Turpentine	Turpentine
VCM	Vinyl chloride
Vinyl carbinol	Allyl alcohol
Vinyl chloride monomer	Vinyl chloride
Vinyl cyanide	Acrylonitrile
Vinylbenzene	Styrene
Vinylidene chloride	Vinylidene chloride
Water-soluble nickel compounds	Water-soluble nickel compounds
Wool process dust	Wool process dust
Xylol	Xylene, *o-,m-,p-* or mixed isomers
Yttrium	Yttrium
Zinc chloride, fume	Zinc chloride, fume
Zinc distearate	Zinc distearate
Zinc distearate	Zirconium compounds (as Zr)
α-Chlorotoluene	Benzyl chloride

REFERENCES

1   The Control of Substances Hazardous to Health Regulations 2002 SI 2002/2677 The Stationery Office 2002

2   *Control of substances hazardous to health (Sixth edition). The Control of Substances Hazardous to Health Regulations 2002 (as amended). Approved Code of Practice and guidance L5* (Sixth edition) HSE Books 2013 www.hse.gov.uk/pubns/priced/l5.pdf

3   General Data Protection Regulation. The Stationery Office 2018

4   MDHS14/4 *General methods for sampling and gravimetric analysis or respirable, thoracic and inhalable aerosols.* HSE Books 2014 www.hse.gov.uk/pubns/mdhs/index.htm

5   *Asthmagen? Critical assessments of the evidence for agents implicated in occupational asthma* HSE 2006 www.hse.gov.uk/asthma/asthmagen.pdf

6   MDHS47/3 *Determination of rubber process dust and rubber fume (measured as cyclohexane-soluble material) in air*

7   The Mines Regulations 2014 SI 2014/3248 The Stationery Office 2014

8   Environmental Protection Act 1990 Ch.43 The Stationery Office 1990

9   *Occupational exposure limits for hyperbaric conditions: Hazard assessment document* Environmental Hygiene Guidance Note EH75/2 HSE Books 2000

10 MDHS59/2 *Machine-made fibres* HSE Books 1988 www.hse.gov.uk/pubns/mdhs

11 *Monitoring strategies for toxic substances HSG173* (Second edition) HSE Books 2006 www.hse.gov.uk/pubns/books/hsg173.htm

12 *Biological monitoring in the workplace: A guide to its practical application to chemical exposure* HSG167 HSE Books 1997 www.hse.gov.uk/pubns/books/hsg167.htm

FURTHER INFORMATION

For information about health and safety visit https://books.hse.gov.uk or http://www.hse.gov.uk. You can view HSE guidance online and order priced publications from the website. HSE priced publications are also available from bookshops.

To report inconsistencies or inaccuracies in this guidance email: commissioning@wlt.com.

British Standards can be obtained in PDF or hard copy formats from BSI: http://shop.bsigroup.com or by contacting BSI Customer Services for hard copies only. Tel: 0846 086 9001 email: cservices@bsigroup.com.

The Stationery Office publications are available from The Stationery Office, PO Box 29, Norwich NR3 1GN
Tel: 0333 202 5070 Fax: 0333 202 5080.
E-mail: customer.services@tso.co.uk Website: www.tso.co.uk.
They are also available from bookshops.

Statutory Instruments can be viewed free of charge at www.legislation.gov.uk where you can also search for changes to legislation.

Notes

Notes

Notes